CREATESPACE AND KINDLE SELF PUBLISHING MATRIX

Disclaimer

Although very possible, there are no guarantees that you will make any money using the ideas laid out within this book. You should not take this to be a "get rich quick" scheme; it requires work and earning potential will be a direct reflection of the abilities, knowledge and work ethic of the individual.

No mention of results or earnings within this book should be construed as a promise or guarantee of similar results or financial gain.

This book is in no way associated with or endorsed by Amazon, CreateSpace or Kindle Direct Publishing.

No authors were harmed during the making of this book.

CREATESPACE AND KINDLE SELF PUBLISHING MATRIX

WRITING NONFICTION BOOKS THAT SELL WITHOUT MARKETING

Chris Naish

CONTENTS

INTRODUCTION

Welcome inside, dear reader,

I'm so excited about this book, and how it is going to help you. You are in for a treat!

First of all, just a few words about me and why I think I qualify to tell you what you should do in regard to your CreateSpace and Kindle books.

I'm lazy here on Kindle…

I don't do pay-per-click (PPC) advertising, and I certainly don't work my butt off promoting my books. (I must try harder!) Still… Every day, day in and day, out my books keep selling and produce paychecks for me each month.

I've had all 3 of my books hit Number 1 bestseller and 2 of those hit this status in 2 different categories. (That's Number 1 in 5 categories if you're as confused as me.)

On top of this, I've been in position #1 and #11 (2 different titles) in the "blogging and blogs" category for books. This covers physical, Kindle and Audible books. Number 1 in the world! (Well… the world of Amazon.com.)

Can you imagine how exciting that felt?

Well, hopefully you won't have to imagine for too much longer because you, my friend, are on the verge of finding out the methods I use. No paying for advertisements, no endlessly chasing interviews from book promo sites, just some good old fashioned (and pretty clever) research methods that I have developed and a couple of neat tricks thrown in for good measure.

If you follow the instructions and take action, I'm sure that at *minimum* you will have the skills to create consistent sales that no "Kindle software," snazzy book cover or brilliant description is going to give you. (Work on that description though, OK?)

Hell, when I started doing this I couldn't even afford a decent cover for my first book but it still sold. I even used Amazon's own terrible cover creator when I first released my second book. Yep... It still sold. (Although it's a good idea to get a half decent cover if you can afford it or once a little money begins to materialize.)

The first thing I want to ask you to do is stop doing what everybody else is doing! Be different, use your head with regard to publishing your book and it will serve you well. In the future, you can think about all the stuff that might or might not work (and take up precious time or money) once you are already earning.

You have brains (or at least determination) on your side; I know this because you are a writer, publisher, author, entrepreneur, or whatever else you want to think of yourself as. Because of this I would like to conclude that you can do what is required of you to make self-publishing work for you. You're not shy about doing a little work, right? Thankfully, it's not as much work as publishing multiple books and never making a cent but that is your choice to make once you have the knowledge.

"Sooner or later you're going to realize just as I did that there's a difference between knowing the path and walking the path."

– Morpheus

Welcome to my book,
Chris Naish

WHO IS (OR ISN'T) THIS BOOK FOR?

First of all, let me tell you what this book isn't. It is not for you if you…

- Write fiction. Although many of the tips will certainly help, you will get more out of this if you are writing nonfiction books.
- Want to learn how to write a book, or want a "book template" to start you off.
- Want to learn how to format your books properly for CreateSpace and Kindle.
- Want to write a crappy book fast and make money forever… Give up on that, junk doesn't sell long term (IMHO)!

You also need to know if this book is compatible with your needs, right?

- Are you willing to spend time researching your niche like a pro?
- Do you want to be able to look at all your competitors

and know exactly where they went wrong when publishing their books? (I don't think you'll want to tell them, but if you do, knock yourself out!)

- Do the concepts behind "search," "keywords," "auto-complete" and "discoverability" on Amazon confuse you?

- Do you want to see a technique that nobody else is teaching before it gets into the mainstream?

- Do you want to hear about *real* Amazon SEO (search engine optimization) that isn't being taught anywhere else?

- Then you are in the right place!

The information laid out in this book is to help the everyday person who has no idea how to market and promote a book to get a real foothold in their chosen niche without an expert's knowledge of sales tactics and other marketing skills. So…

Fasten your seatbelt, Dorothy, 'cause Kansas is going bye-bye…

PART 1:
IDENTIFYING & MINING YOUR COMPETITION

You should learn from your competitor, but never copy. Copy and you die.

– Jack Ma

CREATING A BASE OF GUESSES

"The shrewd guess, the fertile hypothesis, the courageous leap to a tentative conclusion – these are the most valuable coins of the thinker at work. But in most schools guessing is heavily penalized and is associated somehow with laziness."

– Jerome Bruner

(Note: *I'll use these inspirational quotes throughout the book, mainly to give the impression that I'm intelligent. If it doesn't work, please feel free to contact me and let me know. Just be sure to not use any big words.*)

The first step you need to take involves looking at Amazon's own clues about what is being searched for within their site. It's a pretty straightforward process although it does take a little time.

I know…

You've probably already been introduced to all this stuff: auto-complete drop-downs and keywords. OK! The game's up, I swindled you!

Just Kidding!

We'll be going through some basic stuff, but the real magic happens a little bit later, so bear with me!

Now please remember, this is going to be time well spent so please don't skip over any stage when it's time to do this for real.

Let's go...

Think of as many different words as you can that relate to your niche and begin writing them down on a notepad. For my example, I'm using this actual book that you're reading now.

Here are my ideas...

- Kindle
- Publishers
- Publishing
- Writing
- Writers

Now try to combine these individual words into logical phrases that people might use to search on Amazon...

- Kindle publishers
- Kindle publishing
- Writing for Kindle
- Kindle for writers
- Writing on Amazon Kindle

Of course, this should also give you some food for thought for more related searches that could pop up on Amazon. Try to include some questions and statements which may be related to your book as well. Here are a few I've thought up...

- How to publish on Kindle

- How to publish on Amazon Kindle
- How to make money writing for Kindle
- Improve sales on Amazon Kindle
- Promote books on Amazon
- Sell more books on Amazon
- How to sell more eBooks on Kindle

And so on. You can mix and match and add or remove "how to" or any other prefix to a question that is relevant to your niche. These might include prefixes like "where to" in your own particular niche.

FINDING A BASE OF REAL KEYWORDS

First of all, are there other books in your niche already on Amazon? Although not impossible, I would find it very hard to believe that there is nothing already written concerning your niche on Kindle unless you are into writing books on breaking markets. If you cannot find any other books on the subject, you may have a problem. (Then again, you may be onto a goldmine if nobody else has tapped the niche!)

Here's how we start to look up the information on keywords (and more) that we need.

> **Note:** *The following exercises should all be done at Amazon. com (USA) unless you have a special interest in other particular countries.*

- Go to Amazon.com. The left hand side of the search bar will be set to "all." Change it to display "Kindle Store" if you plan on publishing a Kindle book. If you are also planning on publishing via CreateSpace then you can set it to "Books" later when you investigate keywords for your print book.

- Start typing in the phrases that we have created one by one into the Amazon search bar.

- Even before you finish typing in your phrase, you will see phrases that are highly related to your niche appear in Amazon's auto-suggest. Make a note of them, but continue typing in your original phrase as you take notes on what's appearing. It's a stop-start game but as you type each phrase out to completion, more suggestions will usually appear.

- Get rid of anything in your list that isn't producing results in Amazon's auto-suggest. For example, I had "promote books on Amazon" in my original list, but when typed in it produced little of value in the auto-complete so I tossed it! On top of this, don't be afraid to try new phrases as inspiration grabs you while you do this.

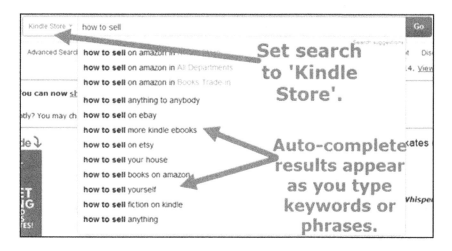

Once you have garnered all the auto-suggest phrases you can from one of your initial "guess" keywords, get rid of it **UNLESS** it appears in the drop-down as you originally wrote it. An example here would be my guess of "how to sell more eBooks on Kindle."

Although it produces many promising auto-complete results, it never appears "as is" so to speak, so I just record the new keyword phrases and dispose of this initial guess.

Here's an updated list of what I found so far:

- **Kindle publishing** (guide/bible/programs)
- **Writing for Kindle**
- **Kindle book research**
- (How to) **Publish on Kindle**
- (How to) **Publish on Amazon** (Kindle)
- (How to) **Publish a Kindle book**
- (How to) **Publish on Amazon** (Kindle)
- (How to) **Publish a book** (on Amazon/on Kindle)
- (How to) **Publish your book** (to Kindle)
- (How to) **Publish an eBook** (on Amazon)
- Promote book
- (How to) **Promote your eBook**
- (How to) **Sell more books** (on Amazon)
- (How to) **Sell more eBooks** (on Amazon)
- (How to) **Sell more kindle** (eBooks/books)
- **Writing nonfiction** (books)
- **How to write nonfiction** (eBooks)

Right, that should do us for starters!

Now take note: The red (or bold if you are reading in black and white) keyword phrases are stand-alone keywords that people type into Amazon's search box. The regular text phrases in parentheses are long tail keyword phrases that have been typed in by Amazons searcher's. You, of course, will be listing them individually – setting them out like this just makes it easier to see all of our options without making our list 4 times longer and more confusing while you read.

If at this stage you are having second thoughts about how practical the use of keyword phrases is, here's a short excerpt from an old but still relevant article by Aaron Shepard: http://www.newselfpublishing.com/AmazonCounting.html

> **"Customers searching and then clicking in results accounted for 31% of detail page visits. While impressive enough in itself, this figure may be deceptively low. The ref codes for Aiming at Amazon (http://www.amazon.com/dp/093849743X) showed that most of the links clicked after a search were for the first book on the first page of results. This suggests that an even higher percentage of customers may reach their first detail page through search results, even if many of them move on from there through Amazon recommendations.**
>
> **Conclusion: Optimizing a book and its listing for search is still the most important means you have to make it visible on Amazon."**

Today, this is what you are going to be learning about, but we are going to take things to a whole new level!

As we continue with our list, the benefits of doing keyword research will become clearer to you once you understand this key concept: *Your book title and the words you specify in the keywords field on the Kindle book upload page both count toward your ranking position in Amazon's search results.*

When Amazon fills out the auto-complete, it is calling on a database of past searches made by other (possibly buying) customers!

The first time this fact dawns on you it is like a revelation, right? The skies open and a blazing ray of light beams down on you... You have been chosen to possess this ancient mystical knowledge. Your world will never be the same again...

...On the other hand, once you've known it for a while it bores you to hell so I'll stop banging on about it for the sake of the sanity of those who already were aware of it.

Ahem! Moving on...

With this knowledge (if it was all I had) I would now roughly draw up a final book name to be something like this:

Title: **Kindle Publishing Guide: How to Publish a Book on Amazon That Sells Itself!**

Subtitle: **Learn How to Sell More Kindle eBooks With Little to No Promotion.**

OK, it's not the most attractive of titles so far but you get the idea, right? A title similar to this is what you might end up with if our research ended here. You might add in a few explosive selling words and all that jazz, but we have more work to do so I'm not polishing our title just yet.

STUCK FOR IDEAS TO START?

It happens, or perhaps you just don't know a great deal about your niche. More likely you want to just cut to the chase, but I suggest you don't on your first run at this. If any of the above circumstances arise, you can use one or more of the tools below to get you rolling. They're free to use.

http://www.keywordtooldominator.com/k/amazon-keyword-tool/

http://soovle.com/ (Make sure you click the little Amazon icon under the search box.)

http://tools.seochat.com/tools/suggest-tool/ (Only check the "Amazon" checkbox.)

Note: *The problem with these resources is that they do not target the "Kindle Store." They look at "all departments," so you will have to verify that any search terms they find appear in the auto-complete after selecting "Kindle Store." Hmm… Never send a machine to do a human's job!*

FIND THE COMPETITION

So now that we have a list of reasonably good keywords to get started on, let's go find out who our competition is and try to beat them all at their own game. MwHa! Ha! Ha! (Sorry about that.)

First things first, get yourself over to http://www.novelRank.com and sign up for an account. Once your account is confirmed and ready to go, head to the "Track Books" page.

Open up Amazon.com in a new tab and one by one, type your keywords into Amazon's search box and hit "Go." Remember to use the "Kindle Store"!

Next start picking out the books that are ranking well (on the first page of results) for each keyword phrase, and that are closely related to the book you want to write.

To avoid confusion, I have included the first 48 results in this demonstration, but you may see page 1 of a search only includes 16 results if you are on a desktop computer. I have done this because you may also see Amazon search pages which include 48 books in 3 columns of 16 on a mobile device or tablet. Likely this is to make the shopping experience easier for those on a mobile device such as their phone, Android tablet, iPad and yes, on an actual Kindle.

The point is, even if you are ranked #48, you are still on page 1 and just a quick swipe of the finger away on a massive number of mobile devices.

SPY ON THE COMPETITION

On each page of Amazon's results:

- Right click on the cover image of the books you are interested in
- Select "copy link location."
- Go to NovelRanks "track books" page.
- In the "Add Your Book to NovelRank" box, use "Ctrl/V" to paste in the URL you just copied into the "Book URL on Amazon" field.

(Those were Windows instructions; I'm not posh enough for a Mac, but I'm sure you Mac users are tech savvy enough to figure it out.)

Hit the "Track Book" button. Once the book is being tracked, delete the used URL from the "Book URL on Amazon" field. Continue to do the same with all the relevant books you find for each of your keywords.

My experience here is that you will keep coming across many of the same titles but keep going through the search process, even if you are only picking out the odd new book now and then. One of these books might help you get found in search hundreds (maybe thousands) of times over a month so it is worth persevering through this process. A little work now can pay dividends for a long time later.

Note: *You cannot add books to NovelRank if they are free, but this doesn't stop you from making a note of these books for later use.*

MINING THE KINDLE BESTSELLERS AND INTERNALLY PROMOTED BOOKS (OPTIONAL)

If you really want to push the boat out, look at the bestseller lists for books that fit your niche in the "Kindle store" at http://www.amazon.com/Best-Sellers-Kindle-Store/zgbs/digital-text/. I encourage you to do so, and I also encourage you to use the "Customers Who Bought This Item Also Bought" and "What Other Items Do Customers Buy after Viewing This Item?" sections on the pages of books you find interesting as you are doing research. I'm not going to drag you through the same process 3 times in 3 different areas of Amazon, but this is an added way to garner valuable information.

A question that might arise for many of you at this point is, "Why don't we just mine the bestsellers instead of going through all that trouble?" Well, you could do that, of course, but you are going to pick up more keywords for your niche if you do it the hard way. Many of these keywords may be a whole lot easier to rank than the ones the big sellers are using. On top of that, every man and his dog are teaching people to mine the bestseller list so... The choice is yours, but if you want to get the most out of this system, it is wise to be thorough.

THE ENEMY

Here is a list of authors we're going to try to beat in this niche, most likely a bunch of nobodies that we will quickly dominate. *Insert evil laugh and air punch here*

Apologies up front for making you read through what is going to be a rather large list, especially if you are reading on your phone, but it is essential that you know exactly what I'm doing and who I'm facing. If I were not giving you training as if you were sitting right next to me and watching my every move, I'd be doing you an injustice.

Without further ado, here are the poor suckers that I'm going to attempt to smash in this particular niche...

Note 1: (eBooks only) *Each author's name links to their author page on Amazon.com (if available), and the book title links to their NovelRank page for that particular book.*

Note 2: *Any grammatical errors in the quoted sections are not of my doing, they are exact copies.*

1. Author(s): Tom Corson-Knowles. Book Title: The Kindle Publishing Bible: How To Sell More Kindle

Ebooks on Amazon (Step-by-Step Instructions On Self-Publishing And Marketing Your Books)

Author of 25 books to date (2 in the list above) and pretty well known among nonfiction (and probably a large group of fiction) writers I imagine.

I've read a couple of this guy's books about Kindle, good stuff from what I've seen so far and worth the investment. (They're not as great as the book you are reading, of course. Given a choice, buying this book a second time would be the intelligent move on your part.)

2. Author(s): Muhammad N. Sikandar. Book Title: Step-by-Step Stupidly Easy Course on How to Make Six Figures Through Amazon Kindle Publishing Exposed – Best Lifetime Money Back Guarantee

A quote from Muhammad's author page: "Muhammad has personally coached hundreds of students to achieve new levels of success with Kindle Publishing by helping them earn 6 Figures in royalties and he charged $1000 per hour for that."

OK, I'll go with $500 per hour if I can beat Muhammad's books sales. ;-)

3. Author(s): Agent* Rick Smith. Book Title: Createspace and Kindle Self-Publishing Masterclass – The Step-by-Step Author's Guide to Writing, Publishing and Marketing Your Books on Amazon

Again, no author page; however, the guy is a Freemason judging by one individual book title and has quite a few other books out. A formidable opponent who knows Kindle publishing judging by the number of books released. There is a "Rick Smith" page, by the way, but it obviously has nothing to do with this agent.

*Note: *If it's not clear why I used the term "agent" above, check this out: https://www.youtube.com/watch?v=QoIXUKTYxyM*

4. Author(s): Norm Schriever. Book Title: The Book Marketing Bible: Essential marketing strategies for self-published and first-time authors, or any writer looking to skyrocket sales.

   Sounds like a friend of mine named Joseph Archibald judging by the blurb on his author's page, also sounds like his books are similar to Adam Shepard's book, "One Year Lived," but I can't say for certain as I haven't read any of Norm's books.

   In all fairness to Norm, I think we are not so much in competition for customers as much as for keywords. Norm's books (aside from the one we are analyzing) are of the humorous autobiography/memoir type unless I have made an incorrect assumption.

5. Author(s): Aaron Shepard. Book Title: From Word to Kindle: Self Publishing Your Kindle Book with Microsoft Word, or How to Format a Text-Only Document in Microsoft Word and Convert to a Kindle eBook

   Pretty much the go to guy for any problem you have with Kindle formatting and I certainly will not be trying to step on his toes in that niche. As far as I'm concerned you can keep that niche, Aaron – it's far too much of an intelligent subject for my liking. I might want some of your keywords though!

6. Author(s): Dr. Andy Williams. Book Title: Kindle Publishing – Format, Publish & Promote your Books on Kindle

The author of 18 books to date and obviously skilled in this trade; just look around Amazon, and you'll see as much. Also seems to have good knowledge of programming, website building and search engine optimization.

7. Author(s): Barb Asselin. Book Title: Write a Kindle Bestseller: How to Write, Format, Publish, and Market a Kindle Bestseller

   Once again I am unfamiliar with this author's work, but here's a quote from her page to give you an idea of her background:

   "Barb Asselin is a college professor and best-selling author who is published in many different genres including education, law, real estate, internet marketing, entrepreneurship, baby sign language, fitness, office administration, children's fiction and children's non-fiction."

8. Author(s): Stefan Pylarinos. Book Title: Kindle Money Mastery: How I Make Six Figures Through Amazon Kindle Publishing Revealed (How To Make Money With Kindle, How To Sell Ebooks)

   In his own words: "I'm an entrepreneur, internet marketer, author, life coach, professional speaker, fitness enthusiast, and world traveller."

   I have had the good fortune to read Stefan's book "Kindle Money Mastery" and I recommend it to you. I'm still going to try to kick his ass, though.

9. Author(s): Michael Rogan. Book Title: Kindle Publishing Made (Stupidly) Easy – How to Prepare, Publish and Promote Your Book Into a Kindle Bestseller

   Not much going on at Michael's page. Inside his book,

however, I found the following information:
"Editor-in-chief Self Pub Nation"

10. Author(s): Ryan Deiss. Book Title: Kindle Publishing Revolution – Amazon Kindle Publishing Guide
A well known and respected internet marketer, I believe Ryan used his considerable leverage to make this book a bestseller when he first released it, and it still sells to this day.

11. Author(s): Cheryl Kaye Tardif. Book Title: How I Made Over $42,000 in 1 Month Selling My Kindle eBooks
Another book I have yet to read, Cheryl has this to say on her author's page:
"I'm an international bestselling Canadian author who loves to say, 'I kill people off for a living!'"
Hmm... Maybe I shouldn't include Cheryl in this book.

12. Author(s): Michael Alvear. Book Title: Make A Killing On Kindle (Without Blogging, Facebook Or Twitter). The Guerilla Marketer's Guide To Selling Ebooks On Amazon
Once again, I've yet to read this book. I found this in the "look inside" of Ryan Deiss's book which should give you an outlook on Michael's thoughts on book promotion:
"You have got to get over the idea that you can sell books on kindle through social media or outside promotion. It is a colossal waste of time."
I have to say, if I have to put a number on it I'm around 80% in agreement with that, but I might have something up my sleeve which proves that statement wrong. (You'll find out about this later!) That said, this

comes across like it will be a very educational read, Michael!

13. Author(s): Paul Stevens. Book Title: Kindle Publishing: The # 1 Killer Proofreading Secret (Steve's Here's How 2!)

Again, a book I have not read. In the blurb area on his author's page Paul lies:

"I would like to say I'm an ex astronaut, have more degrees than a thermometer, have competed in the Tour de France without any EPO, surfed Teahupoo in Tahiti and emerged unscathed, I've sailed round the world, I'm an ace Alpine skier, am a member of Mensa, have a beauty queen wife and gorgeous kids, and started my own corporation which has listed on NASDAQ. I could go on but like Arnold Schwarzenegger I don't want to boast."

Take the lying part light heartedly, you'll have to read Paul's page to see what I mean.

14. Author(s): Ian Stables. Book Title: WHAT MAKES NONFICTION BOOKS BEAT THE COMPETITION?: The special seven step system that almost guarantees a best seller (How to Write a Book and Sell It Series)

Guess what? Right! I've not read this one either! Ian has this to say in his book's introduction:

"This is about what to create so that your book will be amazing. Your book will teach something that gives readers benefits they will not get elsewhere. Not just any benefits, but better ones. They will want your book because it gives advantages other books don't."

I think we are kindred spirits in this belief, Ian!

If you browse further into Ian's "look inside," you'll

find out he is another fan of Michael Alvear and his methods... Bloody hell! That Michael's book looks good! Maybe one day I will go down in legend just as Michael has. *Sigh*

15. Author(s): Martin Crosbie. Book Title: How I Sold 30,000 eBooks on Amazon's Kindle-An Easy-To-Follow Self-Publishing Guidebook

    Here's what the description says on Mr. Crosbie's page: "In a press release, Amazon called Martin Crosbie one of their success stories of 2012. His self-publishing journey has been chronicled in Publisher's Weekly, Forbes Online, and Canada's Globe and Mail newspaper. Martin's debut novel, "My Temporary Life", has been downloaded over one hundred and fifty thousand times and became an Amazon top ten overall bestseller."

    I think we can safely say that this guy seems to know the business very well.

16. Author(s): Laura Pepper Wu. Book Title: 77 Ways to Find New Readers for Your Self Published Book!

    Here is an excerpt from the blurb on Laura's author page:

    "Laura Pepper Wu is the co-founder of 30 Day Books: a book studio. She has worked with a variety of authors to successfully promote their books, including many Amazon best-sellers."

    Another author experienced in what it takes to make a book hit bestseller status.

17. Author(s): Rudy Shur. Book Title: How to Publish Your Nonfiction Book: A Complete Guide to Making the Right Publisher Say Yes (Square One Writer's Guides)

    Rudy has yet to update his author's page but there are

some interesting words from Rudy in the Preface for his book:

"Over the past twenty years, I have lectured to hundreds of writers at colleges and universities throughout New York State. The topic of my lectures? How you can get your nonfiction book published." Undoubtedly Rudy is another expert in this field if he lectures to hundreds on the subject.

18. Author(s): Pam Brossman. Book Title: Self Publish : How to Write A Book in 10 Super Easy Steps (Kindle Boost Series)

Here's what Pam's page has to say about her skill set: "Everyone has an area of expertise that can help another human being get a desired result or outcome in business or in life. Pam Brossman teaches how to access their "unique" strengths and monetize it through the power of technology, digital leverage and highly strategic marketing strategies."

Pam's area of expertise appears to be helping people to learn the benefits of promotion from outside of Amazon.

19. Author(s): Abraham Falls. Book Title: Self Publishing: How To Make Money Online By Self Publishing Ebooks On Amazon TODAY! (Self Publishing, Online Income, Making Money Online)

Abraham has not at time of writing created an author's page. He does, however, tell us inside his book what qualifies him to teach us about sales rank: "Inside you'll discover how to create, publish, and market your ebooks from scratch. These techniques have allowed me to generate my own 5 figure passive income in a matter of months... and it's increasing everyday."

I've not bought this yet, but it is always interesting to learn from those who walk the walk. My wish list is getting bigger by the minute!

20. Author(s): Steve Scott. Book Title: 61 Ways to Sell More Nonfiction Kindle Books

    I have to admit, I have read a few of Steve Scott's books, and they deliver. Here is a small part of what Steve wrote on his author's page:

    "Quality information shouldn't be expensive. The so-called "Internet gurus" love to charge exorbitant prices; knowing this prevents many average folks from achieving success online. What you need (and what Steve provides) is a variety of detailed strategies – Each designed to help you solve a specific Internet business obstacle."

    Yaay! Down with the gurus!

21. Author(s): Steve Scott. Book Title: Is $.99 the New Free? The Truth About Launching and Pricing Your Kindle Books

    Don't get greedy now Steve! I've already sung your praises once already.

22. Author(s): Rob Robideau. Book Title: Kindle Publishing Treasure Map: Simple and detailed guide to making money through Kindle publishing!

    Rob doesn't go into his publishing achievements on his own page; however, the simple fact that he has a book on the subject that sells, along with 5 other books under his belt, does give him some credibility.

23. Author(s): John Tighe. Book Title: Crush It With Kindle – How to self publish your books on Kindle and promote them to #1 bestseller status

Another book that was already on my wish list, I like the look of this one. Here's some of the blurb from John's author page:

"JOHN TIGHE is an online marketing expert, entrepreneur, bestselling author, speaker, business coach and founder and CEO of the Strategic Positioning Press publishing house.

Before striking out on his own John had a career as a corporate lawyer, but decided he wanted more from life. Today, instead of being chained to his desk at a law firm, John works with authors and entrepreneurs from around the world helping them to successfully write, publish and promote their books."

Enough said!

24. Author(s): Alex Foster. Book Title: Write Kindle Books That Sell!: How to find top selling categories for Kindle writing

Quick excerpt from the author page of Alex:

"I hold multiple degrees in psychology, sociology, marketing, business, and my last degree was in pharmacy. I have spent most of my adult life working as a consultant for different health care companies. For a little over the last two years (it's 2013 now) I have been focusing my time on writing books. I love to write about anything I have interest in. Mostly business type books centered around marketing and sales, but also self-help books and even children books."

An experienced publisher with knowledge of marketing, he could be one to watch.

25. Author(s): Edwin Benitone. Book Title: Kindle Publishing Simplified; Better & Faster Ways to Write Kindle Book Within 48 Hours

Edwin also doesn't seem to give a lot away about himself in his book, and there is no author page so I can't put much info here. You're a dark horse, Edwin!

26. Author(s): David Fountaine. Book Title: Kindle How I Published My Book On Amazon

Once again, we have another dark horse in Mr. Fountaine. Come on guys, let us in!

27. Author(s): Mark LeGrand Messick. Book Title: Kindle Marketing: How To Sell More Ebooks On Amazon With Special SEO Tricks (Secrets To Selling Ebooks On Amazon Series Book 3)

Reading from the "look inside" feature on Mark's book it looks like he has similar beliefs to my own with regards to ranking on Amazon. Similar to me, he likes to write in a light hearted, entertaining manner that made me laugh. Not as much as my own writing makes me laugh, however.

I am assuming after a little research that Mark is a follower/student of Steve Scott and a successful one at that. Steve was kind enough to leave a review on Mark's book, and I'll be highly offended if I don't get the same treatment, Steve.

28. Author(s): Mark Coker. Book Title: Secrets to Ebook Publishing Success (Smashwords Guides)

Founder of Smashwords which, in Marks own words: "…is now the world's largest distributor of self-published eBooks. We represent most of the world's bestselling eBook authors, including many NY Times and USA Today bestsellers."

Hmm… Seems to know his stuff, doesn't he? The show-off! Just kidding, Mark. I might be wanting to put this on your site soon so don't be offended!

*Bow... Scrape.

I can tell you that this is an excellent read, by the way, and it's also free (the guy must be rich or something) so check it out.

29. Author(s): Steve Scott. Book Title: How to Write a Nonfiction eBook in 21 Days – That Readers LOVE! *Sigh... I am really going off you Steve; one plug for your books is enough! Throw me that review and I'll put something nice here. Until then p**s off!

30. Author(s): Art Vandelay. Book Title: Self Publishing on Amazon the ultimate guide (Unlimited wealth and happiness awaits)

Art doesn't seem to be very happy at all with the teachings of "snake oil salesmen" on the subject of making money on Kindle judging by the "look inside" feature for his book. I've been down that road too, Art, and it sucks! A few of the guys featured in here might be good reads for you, buddy!

I have yet to read Art's book, but it seems thought-provoking to say the least.

Now... What was I saying before I spent an hour writing, copying and linking (in eBook formats!) all that stuff?

Right! Yes, smashing the nobodies and suckers...

Oh...

My...

God...

I couldn't have chosen a more bloody difficult subject to compete in for my example!

OK, we'll be continuing from here in the "crochet patterns" niche...

Just kidding. I'm quietly confident in my ability... No... really, I am!

Let's move on, but first a quote:

"I choose my friends for their good looks, my acquaintances for their good characters, and my enemies for their good intellects."

– Oscar Wilde

Good! That should help to avert a public lynching.

All jokes aside, the list above will give you an idea of the experience I'm up against in this niche. These are all well known and respected authors, internet marketers and publishers who are writing specifically on the subject matter that they are experts on, "how to publish on Kindle successfully."

USING THE ENEMY AS YOUR MASTERMIND GROUP

"The opportunity to secure ourselves against defeat lies in our own hands, but the opportunity of defeating the enemy is provided by the enemy himself."

— Sun Tzu

Now that we know who we are up against, let's look at their books and see what they are trying to achieve. When you are carrying out the same study of your own niche, the winners may have produced their results by either luck or design. For these guys I am going to assume that much of their success is by design because of the nature of this niche. Hopefully, you will have an easier challenge on your hands than I do!

Let's go to each book's Amazon page and scan over the title looking for more embedded keyword phrases. For all our brainstorming, we are unlikely to have thought of all the angles from which we could approach our niche, so here we are looking at what other successful books in our niche have done.

For my example here I'll take agent Smith's book: Createspace and Kindle Self-Publishing Masterclass – The Step-by-Step Author's Guide to Writing, Publishing and Marketing Your Books on Amazon.

Now, from my original brainstorming I would only have been targeting Kindle authors, but agent Smith has given me quite a helping hand, I now realize I should also be targeting those publishing on CreateSpace!

We have now found a new group of people to buy this book, which I can now tap into by adding a single phrase to my title. Genius, eh?

See what a little research can turn up for you?

Now that we have uncovered this little revelation, we can start investigating more keyword phrases related to CreateSpace. If (and when) this happens to you during your research, once again you should start making a list of all the keyword phrases that are useful as you find them on Amazon's auto-suggest.

- CreateSpace self publishing
- CreateSpace independent publishing platform
- CreateSpace publishing
- CreateSpace and Kindle self publishing

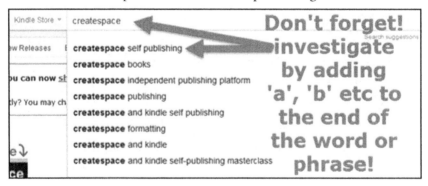

Note: *Although a lot less effective than adding it afterward, adding a letter of the alphabet and a space before a keyword (or*

phrase) can also uncover longer phrases. Just keep deleting the letter and trying the next, working through A, B, C, etc.

Now I'll try to use some of the keywords we had in our previous list, but I'll replace "Kindle" with "CreateSpace."

Erm… Well… Nothing turned up there. And you can wipe that smug look off your face!

It seems like variations on Kindle search requests are far more in demand than their CreateSpace counterparts, but it certainly won't hurt our "discoverability" and hopefully, as a result, our sales to have "CreateSpace self publishing," "CreateSpace and Kindle self publishing" or "CreateSpace publishing" in our book title somewhere.

I'll spare you the pain of seeing me go through all 31 competing titles in this way as it will get boring for both of us pretty quickly wading through pages and pages of this. You should of course work through the titles you find yourself when examining your own niche.

HOW GUESSING CAN RUIN YOUR CHANCE OF SUCCESS

Take another look at the previous image. You'll see in position #7 the phrase "CreateSpace and Kindle."

Let's imagine for a moment that you were to write a book telling people how to format books for both CreateSpace and Kindle. You spend weeks writing your book and in a mad rush to get it out to the world you do no investigation and title your book something like, "Kindle and CreateSpace Formatting Guide for Authors."

Do you see your HUGE mistake?

At time of writing, "Kindle and CreateSpace," does *not* appear in the auto-complete, while "CreateSpace and Kindle" does. If somebody else does it the right way, you lose out on who knows how many potential visitors to your book's page! You would still probably show up in the search results, but the chances are, all other things being equal, that your competitor would show up first.

FINDING OUR STRONGEST COMPETITORS

Each book page we have created at NovelRank will now start harvesting sales information for us. Sometimes you may be lucky and find that books are already being tracked, while at other times there will be no history other than that starting from the date you begin tracking. Here lies our reasoning to find out who your competitors are quickly and get them into the system as soon as you start planning a new book!

Got plans for a new book? Drop everything now and find your competitors as we discussed in the previous steps. The rest of this book can wait!

Now we want to collate some information on each of the books as follows. I will shorten the book titles for simplicity, and also color red and underscore the books that I want to study further.

Anything that doesn't seem to be selling over 1 book a day I have ignored. The average sales per day as measured by NovelRank in this particular niche looks to be around 2 to 3. (NovelRank underestimates, however, so count on it being more!)

Note 1: *If a book has a higher price label and falls under the 1 book a day rule it may still be worth investigating. If a book* *priced $9.99 is selling 1 copy every other day, it is producing way more money than those priced $2.99 that sell 1 copy a day!*

Note 2: *Your niche may be above or below the 1 book a day rule, so use average sales across the board to make your own benchmark. This could also be a point where you identify a niche that isn't profitable enough for you.*

1 – Tom Corson-Knowles: Kindle Publishing Bible **March** Sales: 84 **April** Sales: 48 **Price:** $4.15	**2** – Muhammad N. Sikandar: Stupidly Easy Course **March** Sales: N/A **April** Sales: 25 (in 15 days) **Price:** $3.72
3 – Agent Smith: Self-Publishing Masterclass **March** Sales: 118 **April** Sales: 114 **Price:** $4.10	**4** – Norm Schriever: The Book Marketing Bible **March** Sales: N/A **April** Sales: 9 (in 15 days) **Price:** $9.32
5 – Aaron Shepard: From Word to Kindle **March** Sales: 149 **April** Sales: 131 **Price:** $3.72	**6** – Dr. Andy Williams: Format, Publish & Promote **March** Sales: 19 **April** Sales: 8 (in 15 days) **Price:** $4.42

7 – Barb Asselin: Write a Kindle Bestseller **March** Sales: N/A **April** Sales: 14 (in 15 days) *Gave Barb the benefit of the doubt here as tracking stopped, it was more like 6 days tracked. **Price:** $3.70	**8** – Stefan Pylarinos: Kindle Money Mastery **March** Sales: 41 **April** Sales: 27 **Price:** $3.72
9 – Michael Rogan: Publishing Made (Stupidly) Easy **March** Sales: N/A **April** Sales: 12 **Price:** $3.72	**10** – Ryan Deiss: Kindle Publishing Revolution **March** Sales: N/A **April** Sales: 9 **Price:** $1.24
11 – Cheryl Kaye Tardif: $42,000 in 1 Month **March** Sales: 86 **April** Sales: 55 **Price:** $3.72	**12** – Michael Alvear: Make A Killing On Kindle **March** Sales: 66 **April** Sales: 59 **Price:** $6.40
13 – Paul Stevens: #1 Killer Proof-reading Secret **March** Sales: N/A **April** Sales: 0 (in 15 days) **Price:** $3.67	**14** – Ian Stables: BOOKS BEAT THE COMPETITION **March** Sales: N/A **April** Sales: 10 (in 15 days) **Price:** $3.72

15 – Martin Crosbie: How I Sold 30,000 eBooks **March** Sales: 205 (Possible promos in March?) **April** Sales: 51 **Price:** $5.19	**16** – Laura Pepper Wu: Ways to Find New Readers **March** Sales: N/A **April** Sales: 20 (in 15 days) **Price:** $3.70
17 – Rudy Shur: Publish Your Non-fiction Book **March** Sales: N/A **April** Sales: 0 (in 15 days) **Price:** $13.66	**18** – Pam Brossman: A Book in 10 Super Easy Steps **March** Sales: N/A **April** Sales: 6 (in 15 days) **Price:** $3.84
19 – Abraham Falls: How To Make Money Online **March** Sales: N/A **April** Sales: 21 (in 15 days) **Price:** $3.72	**20** – Steve Scott: 61 Ways to Sell More Nonfiction **March** Sales: 73 **April** Sales: 39 (over 20 days) **Price:** $3.72
21 – Steve Scott: Is $.99 the New Free? **(Book** on free promo from 16th-21st of April 2014) **March** Sales: 133 **April** Sales: 36 (This "low" sales number is caused by the free promo. NovelRank stops tracking until reactivated when a book goes free. Steve's ranking for this book was still very high at Amazon.com at time of writing) **Price:** $1.23	**22** – Rob Robideau: Kindle Publishing Treasure Map **March** Sales: N/A **April** Sales: 11 (in 15 days) **Price:** $4.11

23 – John Tighe: Crush It With Kindle **March** Sales: 55 **April** Sales: 20 (in 11 days) *There was also a problem with tracking switching off; past months show consistent sales however. (See the graph on the bottom of NovelRank page.) **Price:** $4.13	**24** – Alex Foster: Write Kindle Books That Sell! **March** Sales: N/A **April** Sales: 14 (in 15 days) **Price:** $3.72
25 – Edwin Benitone: Kindle Publishing Simplified **March** Sales: N/A **April** Sales: 0 (in 15 days) **Price:** $3.67	**26** – David Fountaine: My Book On Amazon **March** Sales: N/A **April** Sales: 0 (in 15 days) **Price:** $3.73
27 – Mark LeGrand Messick: Sell More Ebooks **March** Sales: N/A **April** Sales: 27 (in 13 days) **Price:** $1.24	**28** – Mark Coker: Ebook Publishing Success **(Book** permanently free) **March** Sales: N/A **April** Sales: N/A **Price:** Free
29 – Steve Scott: Nonfiction eBook in 21 Days **March** Sales: 121 **April** Sales: 120 **Price:** $3.70	**30** – Art Vandelay: Self Publishing on Amazon **March** Sales: N/A **April** Sales: 4 (in 13 days) **Price:** $3.72

IMPORTANT POINTS ABOUT THIS TRACKING

First, the figures given for sales are not exact; NovelRank usually underestimates by quite a bit. What I have read, mixed with experience from tracking my own books, tells me that the greater a book's popularity is, the more NovelRank underestimates. Saying that NovelRank reports around 50% to 60% of sales when talking about the numbers we are dealing with now wouldn't put us too far out, but the idea here is to form comparisons, not measure exact figures, so don't be too concerned about this.

Secondly, NovelRank can't seem to track free books due to the sales rank being for the free Kindle store. Sometimes that can throw a small wrench in the works, but if the book was only on promotion (rather than free indefinitely) you can still garner some knowledge from the graphs at the bottom of its respective page on NovelRank.

If you see a huge number of sales that look out of the ordinary for the niche in general, investigate! There are buttons on each book's page for Twitter and Blog searches which may turn up reasons for high spikes in sales, as well as some excellent ways to promote your own book.

AND THEN THERE WERE 15

So, we have now cut our list down to the 15 books that seem to be getting the most sales in our area of interest. Can we cut this list down more?

Yes, here's what jumps out for me right now…

#21, the Steve Scott book titled: "Is $.99 the New Free? The Truth About Launching and Pricing Your Kindle Books."

- I can find no helpful keyword phrases within this title.
- Low price ($1.23) will also explain the large amount of sales. I'm looking to charge at least enough to hit the 70% ($2.99) payout level with this book. That is obviously possible judging by the other book prices so I don't currently want to estimate what a lower priced book could do for me.
- Steve has a lot of books out; again he likely uses this advantage to advertise this title within other books. Plus we have to factor in the following he has on his popular blog. (Worth reading by the way! http://www.stevescott-site.com/)

14 left…

Next up we want to gather some…

COMMON (OR UNCOMMON?) DENOMINATORS

Let's list our remaining competitors again. Now we want to start extracting even more information that shows us why they are making sales, namely:

- Keyword phrases within the title (broad and phrase match.)
- Categories that they have been listed in and show top 100 ranking for.

While on each book's page, if you can find keywords in the drop-down box while examining the book title then note these down also, along with any ranking the book has for the phrase. Keep pushing Amazon for more information on your niche!

You might not see the following happening in your niche if it is small, but some sought-after books have their title and/or partial matches of their title crop up in the auto-complete. There may be opportunities for this to help you out later so if you spot any, note these down also.

If you know you have already noted down a keyword phrase while examining a previous book, don't bother repeating yourself. Later in the book the reasoning behind this will become clear.

Finally, if you think of any new phrases while doing this exercise and the keywords appear in the auto-complete, feel free to add them at the same time. (For this reason, you may see keywords unrelated to the books below; I'm brainstorming real time as I examine.)

1. Tom Corson-Knowles: The Kindle Publishing Bible: How To Sell More Kindle Ebooks on Amazon (Step-by-Step Instructions On Self-Publishing And Marketing Your Books)

Keywords:
- (The) Kindle publishing (bible)
- (How to) sell More Kindle eBooks
- Self publishing
- Self-publishing (not "self publishing," we missed this earlier!)
- Marketing your book
- Kindle bible

Categories:
- Kindle Store > Kindle eBooks > Education & Reference > Writing, Research & Publishing Guides > Publishing & Books > Authorship
- Kindle Store > Kindle eBooks > Business & Money > Marketing & Sales > Advertising
- Kindle Store > Kindle eBooks > Business & Money > Accounting

2. Muhammad N. Sikandar: Step-by-Step Stupidly Easy Course on How to Make Six Figures Through Amazon Kindle Publishing Exposed – Best Lifetime Money Back Guarantee

Keywords:

- Amazon Kindle publishing

Categories:

- Kindle Store > Kindle eBooks > Business & Money > Skills > Business Writing
- Books > Business & Money > Skills > Business Writing
- Kindle Store > Kindle eBooks > Education & Reference > Writing, Research & Publishing Guides > Publishing & Books

3. Agent Smith: Createspace and Kindle Self-Publishing Masterclass – The Step-by-Step Author's Guide to Writing, Publishing and Marketing Your Books on Amazon

Keywords:

- CreateSpace and Kindle self publishing
- CreateSpace and Kindle
- CreateSpace self publishing
- CreateSpace publishing
- CreateSpace self publishing
- Kindle self publishing
- Kindle self-publishing
- Marketing your book
- Marketing your book on Amazon
- Publishing on Kindle

- Publishing on Amazon
- Publishing your book

Categories:

- Kindle Store > Kindle eBooks > Business & Money > Skills > Business Writing
- Kindle Store > Kindle eBooks > Education & Reference > Writing, Research & Publishing Guides > Publishing & Books > Authorship
- Books > Business & Money > Skills > Business Writing

4. Aaron Shepard: From Word to Kindle: Self Publishing Your Kindle Book with Microsoft Word, or How to Format a Text-Only Document in Microsoft Word and Convert to a Kindle eBook

Keywords:

- Self publishing Kindle

Categories:

- Kindle Store > Kindle eBooks > Arts & Photography > Graphic Design > Design > Books
- Books > Arts & Photography > Graphic Design > Commercial > Book Design
- Books > Computers & Technology > Home Computing & How-to > Microsoft How-to > Word
- Kindle Store > Kindle eBooks > Education & Reference > Writing, Research & Publishing Guides > Publishing & Books > Authorship (extra due to category display change)

5. Barb Asselin: Write a Kindle Bestseller: How to Write, Format, Publish, and Market a Kindle Bestseller

    Keywords:

    - Write a Kindle Bestseller
    - Write a Kindle book
    - How to publish a kindle book
    - Sell more books
    - Sell more Kindle eBooks
    - Sell more eBooks

    Categories:

    - Kindle Store > Kindle eBooks > Business & Money > Skills > Business Writing
    - Kindle Store > Kindle eBooks > Education & Reference > Writing, Research & Publishing Guides > Publishing & Books

6. Stefan Pylarinos: Kindle Money Mastery: How I Make Six Figures Through Amazon Kindle Publishing Revealed (How To Make Money With Kindle, How To Sell Ebooks)

    Keywords:

    - Free kindle eBooks
    - How to sell eBooks
    - How to sell eBooks on Amazon
    - How to sell eBooks on Kindle
    - How to sell more Kindle eBooks
    - How to sell more Kindle eBooks fast
    - How to sell more eBooks

- How to sell more eBooks on Amazon
- Make money with Kindle
- Make money with Kindle books

Categories:
- Kindle Store > Kindle eBooks > Business & Money > Marketing & Sales > Marketing > Web Marketing
- Kindle Store > Kindle eBooks > Business & Money > Industries > E-commerce
- Books > Business & Money > Marketing & Sales > Marketing > Web Marketing

7. Cheryl Kaye Tardif: How I Made Over $42,000 in 1 Month Selling My Kindle eBooks

Keywords:
- Selling Kindle books
- Selling eBooks
- Selling Kindle eBooks
- Selling eBooks on Amazon
- Selling eBooks online
- Selling eBooks on Kindle
- Sell Kindle books
- Sell Kindle eBooks
- Sell more books
- Sell more Kindle eBooks
- Sell more eBooks

Categories:

- Kindle Store > Kindle eBooks > Business & Money > Marketing & Sales > Sales & Selling

8. Michael Alvear: Make A Killing On Kindle (Without Blogging, Facebook Or Twitter). The Guerilla Marketer's Guide To Selling Ebooks On Amazon

Keywords:

- Make a killing on Kindle
- Guerilla marketing
- Guide to self publishing

Categories:

- Kindle Store > Kindle eBooks > Education & Reference > Writing, Research & Publishing Guides > Publishing & Books > Authorship
- Books > Education & Reference > Writing, Research & Publishing Guides > Publishing & Books > Authorship
- Kindle Store > Kindle eBooks > Education & Reference > Writing, Research & Publishing Guides > Writing Skills

9. Martin Crosbie: How I Sold 30,000 eBooks on Amazon's Kindle-An Easy-To-Follow Self-Publishing Guidebook

Keywords:

- Self publishing manual
- Self publishing through Amazon

Categories:

- Kindle Store > Kindle eBooks > Business & Money > Marketing & Sales > Sales & Selling
- Kindle Store > Kindle eBooks > Education & Reference > Writing, Research & Publishing Guides > Writing Skills

10. Abraham Falls: Self Publishing: How To Make Money Online By Self Publishing Ebooks On Amazon TODAY! (Self Publishing, Online Income, Making Money Online)

Keywords:

- Lots of "make money online" keywords, too far from our niche.

Categories:

- Kindle Store > Kindle eBooks > Business & Money > Marketing & Sales > Marketing > Direct
- Kindle Store > Kindle eBooks > Education & Reference > Writing, Research & Publishing Guides > Publishing & Books > Authorship
- Books > Business & Money > Marketing & Sales > Marketing > Direct

11. Steve Scott: 61 Ways to Sell More Nonfiction Kindle Books

Keywords:

- Running out of ideas now… (There are keywords here; we just have them already.)

Categories:

- Kindle Store > Kindle eBooks > Education & Reference > Writing, Research & Publishing Guides > Publishing & Books > Authorship
- Kindle Store > Kindle eBooks > Business & Money > Marketing & Sales > Advertising
- Kindle Store > Kindle eBooks > Business & Money > Accounting

12. John Tighe: Crush It With Kindle – How to self publish your books on Kindle and promote them to #1 bestseller status

Keywords:

- Crush it with Kindle
- How to self publish
- How to self publish your book
- How to self publish on Amazon
- How to self publish on Kindle

Categories:

- Kindle Store > Kindle eBooks > Business & Money > Marketing & Sales > Marketing > Direct
- Kindle Store > Kindle eBooks > Education & Reference > Writing, Research & Publishing Guides > Publishing & Books > Authorship
- Books > Business & Money > Marketing & Sales > Marketing > Direct

13. Mark LeGrand Messick: Kindle Marketing: How To Sell More Ebooks On Amazon With Special SEO Tricks (Secrets To Selling Ebooks On Amazon Series Book 3)

Keywords:
- Kindle marketing
- Kindle marketing secrets
- Kindle marketing magic
- Kindle marketing books

Categories:
- Kindle Store > Kindle eBooks > Business & Money > Marketing & Sales > Marketing > Direct
- Books > Computers & Technology > Internet & Web Culture > Search Engine Optimization
- Kindle Store > Kindle eBooks > Education & Reference > Writing, Research & Publishing Guides > Publishing & Books > Authorship

14. Steve Scott: How to Write a Nonfiction eBook in 21 Days – That Readers LOVE!

Keywords:
- How to write a nonfiction eBook
- How to write nonfiction
- How to write a book
- How to write for Kindle
- How to write a bestseller

Categories:

- Kindle Store > Kindle eBooks > Education & Reference > Writing, Research & Publishing Guides > Writing Skills
- Books > Education & Reference > Writing, Research & Publishing Guides > Writing > Writing Skills
- Kindle Store > Kindle eBooks > Business & Money > Entrepreneurship & Small Business > Entrepreneurship

Note: *If you come across any titles that do not have category rankings, try them again later, but don't fret too much over it. You can also use the "Look for similar items by category" links at the bottom of a books page if you really want to know, or want extra information.*

Phew! Another boatload of keywords for us! Now let's leave the keywords on the back burner for a bit while we look into...

CHOOSING CATEGORIES

Here's where our 13 top sellers are located:

Kindle Store:

- 7 occurrences of: Kindle Store > Kindle eBooks > Education & Reference > Writing, Research & Publishing Guides > Publishing & Books > Authorship
- 3 occurrences of: Kindle Store > Kindle eBooks > Business & Money > Marketing & Sales > Marketing > Direct
- 3 occurrences of: Kindle Store > Kindle eBooks > Business & Money > Skills > Business Writing
- 3 occurrences of: Kindle Store > Kindle eBooks > Education & Reference > Writing, Research & Publishing Guides > Writing Skills
- 2 occurrences of: Kindle Store > Kindle eBooks > Education & Reference > Writing, Research & Publishing Guides > Publishing & Books
- 2 occurrences of: Kindle Store > Kindle eBooks > Business & Money > Marketing & Sales > Sales & Selling
- 1 occurrence of: ~~Kindle Store > Kindle eBooks > Business & Money > Accounting~~

- 1 occurrence of: ~~Kindle Store > Kindle eBooks > Arts & Photography > Graphic Design > Design > Books~~
- 1 occurrence of: Kindle eBooks > Business & Money > Marketing & Sales > Advertising
- 1 occurrence of: Kindle Store > Kindle eBooks > Business & Money > Entrepreneurship & Small Business > Entrepreneurship
- 1 occurrence of: Kindle Store > Kindle eBooks > Business & Money > Marketing & Sales > Marketing > Web Marketing
- 1 occurrence of: Kindle Store > Kindle eBooks > Business & Money > Industries > E-commerce

Books:

- 2 occurrences of: Books > Business & Money > Marketing & Sales > Marketing > Direct
- 2 occurrences of: Books > Business & Money > Skills > Business Writing
- 1 occurrence of: Books > Education & Reference > Writing, Research & Publishing Guides > Publishing & Books > Authorship
- 1 occurrence of: Books > Arts & Photography > Graphic Design > Commercial > Book Design
- 1 occurrence of: ~~Books > Computers & Technology > Home Computing & How-to > Microsoft How-to > Word~~
- 1 occurrence of: Books > Computers & Technology > Internet & Web Culture > Search Engine Optimization
- 1 occurrence of: Books > Education & Reference >

Writing, Research & Publishing Guides > Writing > Writing Skills
- 1 occurrence of: Books > Business & Money > Marketing & Sales > Marketing > Web Marketing

For starters, we can scrap (struck out above) the photography/ graphics categories along with the Microsoft Word category. Not close to our target niche here although there is always the possibility of more books, right? (Not bloody likely; it's all yours, Aaron!)

I also don't like the accounting category; way out again as far as this book's subject matter is concerned and doesn't drill down to its lowest subcategory.

Five of our book choices (at time of writing) appear on page 1 under: Kindle Store > Kindle eBooks > Education & Reference > Writing, Research & Publishing Guides > Publishing & Books > Authorship.

More of our 13 top runners are lurking farther down the top 100 of "authorship," and also a good number of the books that didn't make the top 13!

"Authorship" definitely looks like our best bet for first category choice; a lot of books very similar to our own little book here are very popular in this category, and we also have the potential to do well in the parent categories.

On top of this, "Authorship" is also the lowest possible subcategory available, which is what we want. If we could dig down to another subcategory (for example" > Authorship > Sh**ty Authorship), I would put myself there for additional exposure.

Now we want to be looking at a choice of category that follows an *entirely different path* if possible. We want to stay out of " Kindle Store > Kindle eBooks > Education & Reference" so that we are spreading ourselves into different regions of Amazon for more visibility.

Personally for this book, I like the look of the "entrepreneurship" path of the remaining choices but it can be taken a subcategory deeper:

Kindle Store > Kindle eBooks > Business & Money > Entrepreneurship & Small Business > Entrepreneurship > Startups

Likely a tougher nut to crack, but it gives us a higher ceiling to aim for also! A tougher niche can mean more eyeballs on your book if you can get your foot in the door of the top 100 bestsellers.

But… looking more closely at the categories on Amazon, I'm torn between "Startups" and: Kindle Store > Kindle eBooks > Business & Money > Entrepreneurship & Small Business > Home-Based

Right… Which category is it to be?

You can follow along with my thinking by going here to see figures:

http://www.amazon.com/b?node=154606011 Book categories are listed on the left side with a count of books in each category in parentheses.

I notice that there is another possible subcategory below "Home-Based":

Kindle Store > Kindle eBooks > Business & Money > Entrepreneurship & Small Business > Home-Based > Sales & Selling

At time of writing this category contains only 130 books; this should allow me to get into the top 100 bestsellers for this category almost effortlessly and hopefully on to start ranking in the top 100 for "Home-Based" (4,578 books) and then on to "Entrepreneurship & Small Business" (21,015 books). From there, the sky's the limit so to speak.

Note: *Just to make sure you understand this concept; even though I will try to locate my book in the subcategories "Sales & Selling" and "Authorship" they will still appear in parent categories, and we can still rank in the top 100 for those parent categories. You only gain by drilling down deeper into the subcategories!*

LOCKED IN FOREVER?

One thing to bear in mind here is that you are not forever stuck in these category choices so don't panic if things don't go quite as well as you thought they might have. (Neither should you panic if you have already chosen categories incorrectly for your existing books!)

While we are on the subject, one tactic that can be used to boost sales is to change categories from time to time when sales start to slow down a little. You can play with this tactic too! Placing yourself into more challenging categories when things are going well is another option you have in your arsenal; perhaps you will see an even bigger increase in sales due to extra eyes on your book.

A final point on categories: Sometimes it is difficult to get your book placed where you want it. If this happens to you, when you are selecting your categories in KDP you will see the very bottom check box is "NON-CLASSIFIABLE." Select this rather than attempting to relocate your book, wait for your book to publish, and then use the contact link which you can find on the bottom right of all KDP pages to tell them your problem and request manual placement. Be sure to include the full path you would like your book placed under, like so:

Kindle Store > Kindle eBooks > Business & Money > Entrepreneurship & Small Business > Home-Based > Sales & Selling

Note: *For an easier-to-navigate layout of all of Kindle's Categories you can take a look at this resource which I have put together: http://thinkclickrich.com/Matrix-Categories*

Now… Let's get into the real meat of this book, the stuff you won't have seen before!

PART 2
THE CREATESPACE AND KINDLE SELF PUBLISHING MATRIX

"This is your last chance. After this, there is no turning back. You take the blue pill – the story ends, you wake up in your bed and believe whatever you want to believe. You take the red pill – you stay in Wonderland and I show you how deep the rabbit-hole goes."

– Morpheus

UPLOADING YOURSELF TO THE MATRIX

So now we are aware of a large variety of keywords we might want to target, and we also have a list of the bestselling books related to our niche. Where do we go from here?

We go to our CreateSpace and Kindle Self-Publishing Matrix.

We are now at the part of the book where we find out what really makes our competitors sick (I mean tick!), why they sell with regard to keywords, how many different keywords they rank, and how good the keywords are that they rank for. Then we can use this information to dominate, or at least get a good foothold in the niche when we publish our book.

Just to make things confusing, you have to download the Matrix before you can upload yourself to it. (Trying to make associations to this damn movie is admittedly getting pushed to the limit now!)

Anyway, the Matrix, which I used as a resource for this book, is located here: http://thinkclickrich.com/Matrix-Download.

If you are reading on a phone or a tablet I suggest using your computer for the next section. It will be very difficult for you to follow along unless you can open the Matrix and read at the same time. (Feel free to read on your device while viewing the Matrix on your PC, however.)

Note: *Please refer to the Matrix download as you read the next section or some details may be unclear!!!*

WHAT IS THE MATRIX?

The Matrix is like a freeze frame showing exactly what is going on with regard to the estimated sales, category placement and the keywords each book ranks for (or doesn't rank for) within your niche.

Although the information in the Matrix is fluid and will change from day to day, we can still use our snapshot to draw conclusions. These include our best course of action with regard to category selection, keyword phrase usage, book pricing, finding easy to rank keywords and even to spot promotional tactics that worked for our competitors.

Everybody will experience the Matrix differently; it will look quite different for you and your niche.

THE CATEGORY MATRIX

The first tab on the left when you open the Matrix is our "category examination" tab. We covered this in the section on choosing categories, of course. You can use this model to create your own category Matrix for your niche.

Don't forget, if you can't find any category information for a book you may have to try again later. Depending on your niche, a book's "Amazon Best Sellers Rank" can fluctuate wildly with just a few sales (or lack of them) and send books rocketing up (or down) the rankings.

If you can't find a category, the book may be going through a rough patch regarding sales; it may also be permanently in a rough patch!

When using this part of the Matrix, be sure to take the note found at the bottom of the page into account!

THE KEYWORD MATRIX

The keyword Matrix is located on the second tab on the bottom of the document, and this is where things become really interesting.

> *"I didn't say it would be easy, Neo. I just said it would be the truth."*
>
>   – Morpheus

I know your eyes are just going to glaze over when you first see this, and that's fine. I want to teach you something that will never even cross most self-publishers' minds, and of those who see it, few will ever even take the time to use it to its full potential.

Those that can't be bothered will very likely have the same sales as other "can't be bothered" self-publishers.

To ease your mind, once you have done this for yourself a few times it will become much easier. Make your choice now to do the work before your books are published to ensure you have to do less for a long time when they go live.

Listed horizontally (row 1) you will see all of the books listed in our final 14, I have used the author's surname to denote their book so as to save screen real estate, and also linked the name to the NovelRank page in case you (or I!) need it for any reason.

Listed vertically (column 1), you will find the keywords that we have identified for our niche. Notice that I have colored some keywords in this column red. To become familiar with what this means, be sure to look at the "key" which is located at the bottom of the page (Tab 2 in the Matrix). If you don't know what the colors mean, you may struggle to understand some of the things I say moving forward.

Now that we are on the same page:

When you cross reference a keyword phrase with a book, you will see information in the corresponding field which will show you one of 4 things:

- Green field means that this book does not rank on Amazon's first page (48 titles) of results for this keyword at all.
- Plain white field shows that this book ranks on page 1 but does not contain all of the words within the keyword phrase in its title; the number is its position in the top 48.
- Orange field indicates that this book ranks on page 1 and also contains all of the words from the keyword phrase in its title but not in the correct order; again the number indicates the position in the top 48.
- Yellow field indicates that this book ranks on page 1 for this keyword and has the *exact* same keyword phrase within the book title. The number (as usual) gives us the ranking position.

An example: On row 119 we have the keyword phrase "Sell more Kindle eBooks." When I went to Amazon.com, set the search category to "Kindle Store" and then typed in the above phrase, I got the following results for our top 13 books: (Note, these results are, of course, subject to change as rankings change over time.)

- In position 1 was Tom Corson-Knowles, the keyword was a phrase match with his book title: The Kindle Publishing Bible: How To *Sell More Kindle Ebooks* on Amazon (Step-by-Step Instructions On Self-Publishing And Marketing Your Books). Do you see how our keyword phrase appears in the book title *exactly*? (Highlighted yellow in the Matrix)
- In position 5 I found Mark LeGrand Messick's book. This time there was a broad match for the keyword with his title of: *Kindle* Marketing: How To *Sell More Ebooks* On Amazon With Special SEO Tricks (Secrets To Selling Ebooks On Amazon Series Book 3)
- Notice how all the words from our keyword phrase appear in the title? They do not, however, appear in the correct order, which gives us an example of a broad match for a keyword phrase. (Highlighted orange in the Matrix)
- Finally, in position 7 I found Steve Scott's book: 61 Ways to *Sell More* Nonfiction *Kindle* Books. Note that the word "eBooks" is not in the title at all, although it is close. (Plain white in the Matrix which denotes a partial match)

"Jesus. What a mind-job."

– Cypher

From this example, I hope you can see the importance of the order of the words in your book's title. Look throughout the Matrix, and you will see that rankings are based in a world that is built on rules. One such rule is that phrase matches will outrank broad matches, and broad matches will outrank partial matches.

There will be exceptions, of course. I'm not going to pretend that I know everything about the Amazon algorithm – they are guarding all the doors and holding all the keys – but a few of the factors that might help to overrule the norm in this particular instance are items like:

- Reviews.
- Refund percentage.
- Previous or current sales levels.
- Conversion rate when a visitor lands on a book's page.
- Conversion rate when a visitor lands on a book's page for a particular keyword phrase.
- The price. (Amazon makes more money from higher priced books)
- More importantly for us, the 7 keywords you wish to include in KDP (or 5 in CreateSpace) when you upload your book will certainly have a bearing on its ranking. More on that later, however.

TAKE THE RED PILLS, TAKE THEM ALL!

What we are going to do now is select the keywords we want to use for this book. You will find the best (red pill) keywords listed at the bottom left side of the Kindle Matrix. These are more keywords than we can use as a phrase match in one book title, obviously, but if I cannot use all of them in the book title then I can use them later as you will find out.

The keywords listed as "red pills" are likely to get the most eyes on your book via search, *especially if you rank well for them*. Why? It takes very little typing into Amazon's search box to make these words appear in the auto-complete drop-down. This tells us that they are popular search terms that Amazon tries to "bring up" for visitors quickly. Everything in the auto-complete will, of course, bring you traffic to some degree if you rank for it, but the biggest searches are the ones that appear first on the auto-complete!

Let's see if we can prove this point...

Go to the search box (set to Kindle store) on Amazon and type "how to." The first phrases you see are entirely unrelated to our niche (and more popular than our niche, of course!) When you add a letter "p," however, two possible keywords for our book appear: namely, "how to publish a book" and "how to publish an eBook."

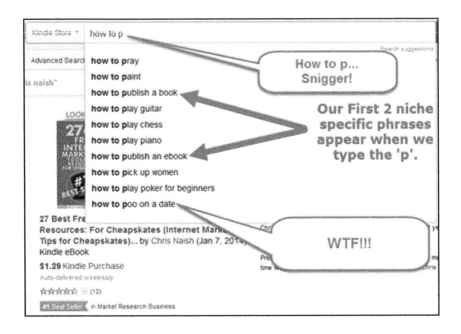

We now have a reason to include these phrases in our red pill keywords. I have only used "how to publish a book" as a red pill because it appears first in the drop-down. Because it appears first, it indicates to me that it has more search queries than "how to publish an eBook."

Be sure to identify the red pill keywords in your own niche! You will find that many similar phrases can be found, but in general it is wise to go for the ones that appear first if you want maximum exposure.

Next let's examine the best sellers (units sold) among our final 14 books. (See the Matrix)

GETTING INFO FROM THE BOOK RANKED #1

Aaron Shepard ranks Number 1 with "Write a Kindle Bestseller: How to Write, Format, Publish, and Market a Kindle Bestseller," (well done, Aaron!) but I do *not* believe that Aaron's sales are the result of great Kindle keyword research in this case. For those of you that know of Aaron, you will also know that he has several books out in this niche, likely linking to each other for increased sales.

The book's keyword ranking is mediocre compared with many of the titles in our top 14 but will obviously help sales. The only phrase match is "self publishing" which comes late in the title along with only 2 broad matches.

Here, I would credit Aaron's popularity, ability to publish great books and the internal linking of said books for the sales of this particular title.

GETTING INFO FROM THE BOOK RANKED #2

Steve Scott comes in at #2 for sales and once again he is a very popular author with multiple books in this niche. This leads me to believe that some sales are the result of purchases made from referrals from within his own library, and from his website.

The second reason I think keyword research is not responsible for significant sales here is because Steve has not directly targeted the red pill "writing nonfiction" with his title.

Steve ranked #4 for the term "writing nonfiction" at time of writing; the #1 position is held by a book called "Writing Nonfiction, 5th Edition: Turning Thoughts into Books." It may be that this book came before the search term "writing nonfiction" or after. It's hard to judge this as the search may or may not be directly for the book itself. Either way we can look into incorporating this search phrase into our own book. I am going to deduce that Steve's other traffic methods help him to build up sales for this title, so this is likely not going to be one of my main targets although I will at least *try* to get the words "writing," and "nonfiction" into my title somewhere!

The second red pill phrase that Steve's book is ranking for is "how to write a book." I got a little surprise at this point because I like the guy who ranks #1 for this phrase, (and I had never seen the book before now) – take a bow Mr. Peter Garety! Here's his book:

How To Write A Book: 3 Steps To A Perfect Outline For Your Book Even If You Have No Idea Where And How To Start. (Peter usually gives out some good info, so this interests me. Sorry to digress, but this is relevant!)

I suspect that the search term "how to write a book" was in existence before Peter's book was published in this case. Peter is pretty sharp so maybe he isn't letting on that he is as good as he is at Amazon keyword research just yet. Note, however, that the phrase match is placed right at the very beginning of his main title, hence the Number 1 ranking.

Are you getting some ideas here on how you can keep deepening one of your existing Matrices or adding new Matrices?

The Matrix method of research for CreateSpace and Kindle publishing is not only vital to the success of the book you are currently working on, but it may provide you with ideas for future successful books! Also, when self-publishing becomes more competitive, in-depth research methods akin to those contained within these pages will be one of the few ways to beat most competition without resorting to paid advertising.

If there is one part of this book you should make a note of, it is the above 2 sentences. They bear repeating:

"The Matrix method of research for CreateSpace and Kindle publishing is not only vital to the success of the book you are currently working on, but it may provide you with ideas for future successful books! Also, when self-publishing becomes more competitive, in-depth research methods akin to those contained within these pages, will be one of the few ways to beat most competition without resorting to paid advertising."

– Chris Naish

Sorry, had to get at least one quote from myself in here.

Moving on…

Now that should blow your mind if nothing before this has. The Matrix is also a place where you can find successful book ideas before you even finish the one you are researching!

Going back now to Steve's book: In our "ranking and sales totals" area of the Matrix, Steve only ranks for 10 different keyword phrases which is on the low side compared to many in our final 14. What does this prove? It proves that Steve has a promotional model quite different from the one I am teaching you (multiple books in a niche, and subscribers in his list) which you should not ignore.

"This is a money digging world of ours; and, as it is said, 'there are more ways than one to skin a cat,' so are there more ways than one of digging for money."

– Seba Smith

NOW IT GETS INTERESTING... THE BOOK RANKED #3

Well, well... We both would have thought that we would have learned the most from the bestseller (or at least #2) in our niche, right? We now come across one of our biggest lessons in Kindle publishing...

Agent Smith jumps in with the third best sales at 3.8 sales per day. The book costs a little more ($4.08) than almost all of the other books in our final 14 and yet he still outsells them. What does that tell us?

Smith is doing something that no other author in our niche is doing... You remember, right?

He also targeted CreateSpace!

What else?

Go look at the Matrix again. Agent Smith ranks for 26 different keyword phrases in a broad match, 5 in an exact phrase match, and another 10 which he ranks for because "some" of the keywords are in the title, or possibly in the 7 keyword options on the book upload page.

Now that is a recipe for success that needs little to no promotion!

The nice looking cover and great description also help as you might deduce, as does the size of the book (236 pages!) but we have also found a big difference that has set him apart from the crowd.

The biggest seller is not necessarily the person you should be worried about emulating when using the Matrix method. The author could be running ads or have his own group of books promoting himself. It is the intelligent (lucky in some cases?) author using Amazon SEO that you need to emulate... and then crush! (That "crush" bit wasn't really necessary, but it felt good when I was writing it.)

Note: *This is exactly why you should be wary of software programs that tell you to copy a book simply because it is the top seller in a particular niche, category or for a certain keyword phrase. Does the software or system take into account external promotion?*

To begin with, agent Smith has no other books in this niche.

Secondly, from what I can see on the Twitter and blog search on NovelRank, there have been no big promotions during the period he made these sales. I may be wrong here, of course – agent Smith may be throwing Facebook ads or something else out there to promote sales, but I doubt it. Sales during March and April were remarkably similar and didn't beat our top sellers, which you might expect if outside influences were at work.

Trinity – "What's he doing?"

Morpheus – "He's beginning to believe."

Note: *With regard to naming your book, when looking for people to emulate in CreateSpace and Kindle publishing, look for consistency. Identify and avoid emulating books that have large rankings/sales due to outside influences!*

Let's take these phrases from agent Smith and move on:

- CreateSpace
- CreateSpace self publishing (which includes the previous keyword but agent Smith only ranks with a broad match!)

From here, I'm going to tell you right now that these 2 keywords are going to be a part of my title, exact phrase match if possible and very early in the title. They seem to be helping agent Smith so hopefully they will return dividends for us too.

Our next bestseller at (joint) #4 is Cheryl Kaye Tardif. I don't believe that the majority of Cheryl's sales come from keyword discovery; I think Cheryl's expertise lies in promotion and marketing elsewhere. With that said I would like to hedge my bets and try to rank for the same 3 broad terms as Cheryl does but my priorities lie with the red pills. Cheryl's broad match keyword phrases were:

- Selling eBooks
- Selling Kindle Books
- Selling Kindle eBooks

The final book I'll look at here is Tom Corson-Knowles at #5. If you look at the Matrix you will see that Tom ranks for an astonishing amount of broad searches (33 that we know of). This is what I also want to do to get maximum exposure throughout searches for terms related to our niche.

Note: *I have taken the other books into account, but I don't want to keep repeating the process here. I'm sure you have picked up the idea.*

PART 3
CREATING A BOOK THAT SHOWS UP EVERYWHERE!

"Visibility creates opportunities"

– Dan Schawbel

Now, let's write a title that takes the best keywords of our competitors and uses the maximum number of red pills. Remember that sales from some books are going to be higher simply because the author either has his own methods of promoting inside of Amazon, or perhaps is very skilled at external promotion. We don't really want to emulate the keyword phrase selection of experienced external promoters. We are better off looking at those who have above average sales and rank well for red pill keywords.

Once these books are identified, we can integrate their keywords into our campaign as well as trying to include other red pills from the niche. The bonus here is that if we do not use them for our current book, they are there in our Matrix waiting for our next book in this niche (if we choose to write more books on the subject), or for a change in our KDP keywords in the future.

So here's what I'm looking at for the title...

- Main title: CreateSpace and Kindle Self Publishing Matrix – Writing Nonfiction Books That Sell Without Marketing
- Subtitle: Publishing an eBook on Amazon Kindle Publishing or CreateSpace Self Publishing How to Guide
- Series title: How to Write a Book for Kindle and CreateSpace Publishing

Note: *View the tab marked "Title Brainstorming" in the Matrix to see the process of including red pills in your own titles. Color important red pill phrases red as you write so you don't remove them accidentally when playing with the title. Also mark any matches as "phrase" or "broad" on the left depending on what match type you managed to fit in. It can become confusing if you don't use a system like this!*

Note2: *If you find your title is cut down by Amazon (see image below) you have overdone the length of your titles! As this was my first time using such a horrid title, I found out about this shortly after publishing the book. If the same thing happens to you, shorten the series title as you will likely have your main and subtitles on your cover.*

CreateSpace and Kindle Self Publishing Matrix - Writing Nonfiction Books That Sell Without Marketing: Publishing an eBook on Amazon Kindle Publishing or ... CreateSpace Publishing Print on Demand 1) [Kindle Edition]
Chris Naish ☑ (Author)
★★★★★ ☑ (8 customer reviews)

I know what you're thinking! That's a hell of a long title, right? (It was longer, look at the Matrix later to see my initial mistake.)

It is, and I wouldn't normally go with something quite so long but this book is here to prove a point on keyword phrase inclusion within titles, so I have to try to get as many red pills into the title as possible. This is the only way you, the reader, can measure the effectiveness of what I am teaching here. Understood? (I'll try not to be so gung ho with my keyword phrases in future books!)

Note: *Please read this new information at my site, on why you shouldn't keyword stuff your titles. This is a very important update since this book was first published!* http://thinkclickrich.com/Kindle-Keyword-Stuffing.

There is a video I will direct you to later in this book showing how fiction writers are doing this kind of thing and getting additional traffic, although not as effectively as we are. Oh, and trust me when I say I hate this book's title more than you do!

Moving on, here's something you need to remember: You must keep the main title and subtitle to fewer than 200 characters (including spaces) as this is the most Amazon will allow us. This does not include the series title, but I recommend keeping all of the titles under 200 characters so that your title isn't cut down like mine was! (There's a lesson to be learned every time you make a fool of yourself eh?)

SUGAR COATING YOUR RED PILLS

I'm not going to be a hypocrite and tell you not to do as I have done, but if you want to make your books look more professional with regard to the title then identify the best red pills and try to use longer phrases from your Matrix that include those red pills.

As an example, the red pill keyword phrase "self publishing" is included in quite a few other longer phrases within the Matrix:

- Self publishing Amazon
- CreateSpace and Kindle self publishing
- CreateSpace self publishing
- Self publishing guide

And so on. We can also use the last word of this red pill (publishing) as a launch pad into new phrases such as:

- Publishing an eBook on Amazon
- Publishing for Kindle
- Publishing your book

There are hundreds of examples just in our Matrix, but can

you see how easy it is to build a title that includes a red pill and a few longer keyword phrases by sugar coating the red pill? Here's an example:

- CreateSpace self publishing guide

Yes, it's basic but you have quadrupled your exact phrase keywords with…

- CreateSpace
- CreateSpace self publishing
- Self publishing
- Self publishing guide

…while using the red pill.

If you never rank well for the red pill, you have a backup in place by hedging your bets on a few other phrases. You will of course include more than 3 when you take into account your subtitle and (optionally) series title. This still doesn't take into account all the broad phrases you will pick up; remember how many of those Tom Corson-Knowles ranked for!

To find longer "sugar coated" versions of your red pill keywords in your own Matrix, simply hit "Ctrl" + "F" and then type the red pill in.

GET YOUR UNIQUE ANGLE

As well as bare keywords within our title, we want to give some sort of uniqueness to our book. I did this by taking the "Matrix" angle. You may or may not be able to use a similar strategy for your niche but it is good to bear in mind that you should attempt to stand out from the crowd in some way.

A unique angle will also allow potential readers looking for your book specifically to find it more easily in search.

EXPLOIT PAIN AND PROBLEMS

Look at where you can solve somebody's problem and integrate this into your title. In this book's title(s) I let the potential reader know:

- I'm going to show them how to sell books.
- They will not have to do a lot of promotion to achieve this.

And while I was telling them all this, I was also integrating "sugar coated red pills" and more keyword phrases into the title(s), of course.

PULL OUT ALL THE STOPS!

Look at the Matrix once again. To the right side of the "key" you will see a list of must use keywords. This list is pretty self explanatory but below the must use keywords there are secondary words and stop words that are popular in our list of keywords.

Some of these stop words will naturally appear in the keyword phrases that you use in your books but some, of course, will not. If you can work them in somewhere, you can increase your chances of showing up in more broad searches and in a higher position.

If you find that your title(s) have the same stop word multiple times, it is a good idea to replace one of these occurrences with another choice if possible. Just *be sure that you are not breaking any phrase matches you had in place when doing this!*

THE 7 FALLEN ANGELS

When it's time to upload your book to KDP, one of the options you have is to include 7 different keywords related to your book. Once you have created your title, you should have a list of the keywords you managed to include with a phrase match (your title brainstorming tab), right?

You also have a list of keywords you simply couldn't fit into your title, as much as you wanted to. These are your "fallen angels" and you only get to choose 7, so which 7 should it be?

Note: *CreateSpace only allows 5 different keyword phrases and these should be mined from the "books" auto-complete search.*

At time of writing, I don't recommend you use keyword phrases that you already have in your title or subtitle exactly and neither does Amazon! (See image below) This is a waste; instead try to use keywords that are not included in your title at all.

The less related (with regard to word similarity) they are to your title, the better in my opinion. Once again this is going to give you more discoverability, as you will also rank for similar keywords to the ones you upload.

Note: *If you choose, you can make an exception to the rule of using unrelated keywords in the keyword field in order to support red pills in your series title. This is because the series title doesn't give great results in most cases and needs a little help from the keyword field.*

Search keywords   ×

Search keywords help readers find your book when they search the Kindle Store. You may enter keywords or short phrases that describe your book and are relevant to its content. The best keywords are those that do not repeat words in the title, category, or description, as these are currently already used to help readers find your book. Some types of keywords are prohibited and may result in content being removed from sale. Click here to learn more.

Conversely, you may also want to try for a broad match on some of the easier to rank keyword phrases that you couldn't get into your title. You can find these by looking for a straight green row with nobody ranking with "phrase match" in your Matrix. An example on our Matrix would be the phrase "How to write nonfiction eBooks" on row 43.

Another thing to bear in mind if you use red pills is that if there is a lot of competition in your niche for this particular red pill (lots of people using it in titles), then using it as one of your fallen angels might not give you results. A longer tail of the red pill might, however!

That's my take on how to begin. You will likely have a whole bunch of keywords you would like to put in place, but can't find room. The thing to remember here is that once again, you are not locked into the first 7 keywords you make use of. You can update this field with different keywords later. Once you have had your initial launch, and things begin to settle into a regular routine of sales, you can start swapping out keywords if some are not performing for you. (Check your position in the search results!)

Finally, give it *at least* a week before you make a decision to change up your keywords once again. The only thing I have seen by rashly changing keywords all the time is a *loss* in sales, and you don't know what is causing it because you have messed around so much! Play it cool, give things a week at least, and only change 1 thing at a time so you can monitor what has actually worked – or what hasn't.

WHERE ELSE TO PUT YOUR SUGAR COATED RED PILLS?

I'll go into this more a little farther on, but I'm not a big believer in using the description for boosting your keyword rankings, at least not at this time of writing. That doesn't mean you shouldn't use them, however, as they may help, but this has more to do with search engine optimization for Google etc., rather than internal ranking boosts within Amazon in my experience.

In my opinion, you should be more concerned with doing a good job of converting browsers into buyers with your description. Many of your keywords will usually show up in your description anyway, so don't try to force it. Nothing puts people off a book faster than a description that doesn't make sense or read naturally, because the author has forced keywords in.

STEALING YOUR COMPETITOR'S POTENTIAL READERS?

Here's a quote from the description of Glyn Williams book, "Bestseller Tactics: Self Publishing techniques to help you sell more books on Amazon and make more money. Advanced Author Marketing"

"You've probably bought the *Self Publishing Bible* books by Tom Corsen Knowles, read John Tighe and his *Crush it with kindle*, studied Derek Doepker and his *Kindle Bestseller Secrets*, and maybe read John Locke with his story of self publishing and selling a million ebooks. They are all very fine books."

Now, why on earth would any author cite other authors and their "fine books" within his description? Surely this is a great way to lose sales by giving good references to others. You want the visitor solely focused on you and your offering, not the books of a competing author, right?

Look again, and notice the italicized keyword phrases. (They are italicized above and on the book's page.) I believe that this author is trying to sell more copies of his own book by piggybacking off the success of others. Start typing any of these book titles (or author names for that matter) into Amazon and you will see them appear in the auto-complete. These books (and authors) are so popular that they are searched for by name. Including them in the description can only result in a little extra traffic, surely!

Now, go type these phrases into the Amazon search box and see if you can find this Glyn Williams book. Look as far past page 1 as you like. Any luck?

Let's try another experiment…

Amazon's search algorithm is, of course, different from "typical" search engines such as Google, Bing, and Yahoo. I would like to put forward the idea that with regard to ranking keyword phrases in Amazon, it is almost useless to use them in your description. This is obviously not the mainstream view (and certainly not my own until I was carrying out research for this book), and I'm sure it will put a few noses out of joint as bloggers and "experts" all over the internet and in Kindle books are telling us different. I can already see the 1 star reviews proclaiming I am wrong!

"I read up until the point where he talks about book descriptions, and then I immediately stopped reading and gave this 1 star review because I am not an open minded person.

The author introduced a new way of thinking and I don't like change! Terrible, save your money and read the same repeated drivel from websites in this niche!"

Well, let's hold off on the stone throwing for just a second while I try to prove my point.

Let's take a look at agent Smith's description for his book "CreateSpace and Kindle Self-Publishing Masterclass." You will notice that in his description, the second heading says, "**Probably the Most Complete New Author Guide on the Market Today**." Type this sentence into Amazon search and it turns up *NOTHING*! Maybe the search is too long? Try "**new author guide**," this returns results but Smith's book is nowhere to be found. Surely having a "phrase" in a description header counts for something, enough to at least get Smith on the map? It seems not!

OK, you got me! These are not keyword phrases that appear in the Amazon auto-complete, perhaps that is why? A little bit further down agent Smith's page however we see the phrase "**marketing 101**" in one of the headings. Where does Smith land in the rankings for this? NOWHERE! Not seen *at all* in 29 pages of search results.

What does show up in there? "Handbag Designer*101*: Everything You Need to Know About Designing, Making, and *Marketing* Handbags," I rest my case.

This tells me that Amazon does not use its book descriptions within its algorithm as many suppose it does. If Amazon uses the description at all, it seems to be of little consequence when compared to other factors. If Amazon's search engine worked in the same manner as Google, we would have had agent Smith's book in the results of all of these searches.

Note: *This may not have always been the case. In the past, authors may have been quite correct in including "Amazon's keywords" in the description, I am just speaking from what I find now.*

Now type the same sentence I originally mentioned, "**Probably the Most Complete New Author Guide on the Market Today**" into Google, what do you see? I get agent Smith's book back in first position.

So, what does this teach us?

The keyword research we do for our title and keywords when uploading may *not* be the best keywords to put into our description. It also doesn't seem to work for piggybacking off the traffic of best-sellers in a niche as you will see many authors trying to do.

Because the searches made on Amazon are not the same as the searches made on Google, we should be doing a different kind of keyword research for our descriptions if we want to get additional traffic from the search engines. This will be a familiar theme for those experienced in SEO and internet marketing and they will realize the potential here for the inclusion of long tail keywords within their description and many other areas of their book(s) page that are under their control, such as:

- More about the author.
- Editorial reviews.
- From the author.
- From the inside flap.
- From the back cover.
- About the author.
- Customer reviews. (You didn't hear me say that!)

If you are going to go down this road, I will recommend very long tails which have little competition. Why? Because the long tail (usually) includes the head keyword anyway. If Google doesn't rank your Amazon page(s) well for the head keyword, you may be able to get a little traffic for the long tail. That's a subject for another book (insert blatant plug for my keyword research book here) however!

A VIDEO OF INTEREST

Right now I'd like to point you in the direction of the video that demonstrates just how effective the correct keyword placement within titles can be. If you would like to skip some of the initial niceties and hear what this author (and others) did to power up his sales, start from the 11:55 point.

http://bit.ly/AmazonKindleKeywords

Please take note of the mention of Amazon's new take on this practice!

Can we take advantage of this to piggyback off the success of other authors? Yes, in theory we could, but I wouldn't suggest you do it directly by putting another author's name or book title in the 7 keywords you upload, or in your titles. You are asking for trouble by doing this. If the other author complains, or if an Amazon rep catches on to what you are doing, you might find yourself with a smacked wrist.

If you were a clever so and so, however, what you could do is have the same words as the author's title within yours in a broad sense which would likely land you quite high in search results for the book in question.

I could, for example, throw the word "bible" or "crush" into my title somewhere and show up in search results for Tom

Corson-Knowles or John Tighe's books, but I prefer originality in this area, even if I am prepared to leech off the success of other authors with regard to my research. I suggest you do the same; a blatant and direct rip-off of sales from an author's hard earned brand or name recognition is just not the way to go in my opinion.

SEEING THROUGH THE INVISIBLE HAND (PRICING)

I'm sure you are expecting something in depth and boring here, right? Well, thankfully it's a quick section and pretty simple to work with. After you have done the work of creating your Matrix and set up tracking for your enemies, usually you will pretty much have all the information you need.

The great thing about the Matrix research method is that you don't have to be an expert with pricing strategies as you already have several models to guide you. Those models are the best sellers in your niche.

My suggestion is that you start at the lower end of the scale or even under it to get your sales levels up and a few reviews in before you start testing out higher pricing. There will be exceptions when you may want to reduce your price to the bare minimum, however, such as:

- First book of the series.
- Products you want to sell via internal links to an offer page. (Note that I didn't say put affiliate links in your book, because this is a very grey area! Read section 5.1.2 here: https://kdp.amazon.com/terms-and-conditions)
- Signing up readers to an email list.

This is just off the top of my head, I'm sure you can think of more.

In the bonus section, you will also find a tip that lets you know by email automatically when your competitors are doing really well with regard to sales rank. If this is due to pricing strategy you will know about it and then you can copy its success!

To cut a long story short, if your niche is already in existence on Amazon, the market will already hold the clues as to what customers are willing to pay for the product. There is nothing stopping you from giving added value in some way so that you can raise the bar on pricing, however!

COVER, CONTENT AND DESCRIPTION DESTROYING ALL YOUR HARD WORK?

Although you don't really need to spend an enormous amount of money on a cover, if you have the funds it is best to get something that will at least stand out from the crowd of people using Kindle's own cover creator to start with. Fiverr.com has some talent in this area as you have no doubt heard before. Even if their covers don't blow people away, at least they don't look like run of the mill covers made by the Amazon cover maker.

Once a book is earning, you can use some of that money to upgrade. I decided to pull out all the stops for this book and used a company called DamonZa.com (http://thinkclickrich.com/ DamonZa) for cover creation. You can see for yourself the results you get back when you have an award winning cover creation team in your corner. (Thanks for the recommendation, Belinda!)

With regard to your description, please don't use a crappy 4 line blurb with misspellings, written in broken English, and then come back to me saying this system doesn't work and nobody is going to buy that book no matter how well you have done your homework! If you are unsure of what you should put in your description, look at what is working for other authors that sell well in your niche and use this for inspiration and to educate yourself.

If English is not your first language, take the time to *at least* have a friend whose first language is English go through your product and correct glaring mistakes. Better still, call on a proofreader to do the job for you if funds allow.

As excited as you will be to get your book out there and earning once it is finished, spend some time on the two points above. Don't fall at the last hurdle! You might "lose" a month's worth of your Amazon payments doing this, but you increase the chance that there will actually be payments to begin with.

Finally, your book's content itself must be good. I have 99-cent books out there that are less than 20 pages long, not filled with loads of stuff but what is inside is of great value if used wisely and it is set at the right price! I also have books that are more expensive, much longer and have images to help the reader learn. The one thing you must try to do is give the reader their money's worth and then some. Failure to do this will result in bad reviews and guess what? Nobody is going to buy a book with a bunch of bad reviews. Game over, and all your hard work goes down the chute.

Finally, if funds allow get a proof reader/editor and somebody who can format your work to make it look good. To this day I've been guilty of skipping this in favour of a DIY approach but I'm now hearing about errors here and there from readers and reviewers so I am in the process of having all my books looked at. Here are the people that I trust to do a good job on this for me and at a fair price:

- Proofreading /editing: Lorecee from http://thinkclickrich. com/Proof-Edit
- Formatting: Lis from http://thinkclickrich.com/ Book-Formatter

Do a good job with your content and it will continue to produce income for you. The extra work and cost are worth the trouble!

PART 4
BOOK PROMOTION & REVIEWS

"Without promotion something terrible happens... Nothing!"

– P.T. Barnum

In this section, I will show you exactly how lazy I have been with book promotion outside of Amazon itself.

Pretty dumb for me to make such a statement after you bought this book, which is trying to tell you how great I am at helping you to sell more books, right?

Well no, not really!

I told you in the intro I was lazy about many things, and with regard to external promotion that is very true. You see that I do all the work up front so that I don't have to mess around with promotion too much. This is great news for you, because if I can make money in my own lazy manner then you are going to do better if your marketing skills are up to scratch.

If you know a lot about marketing and promotion anyway then please feel free to skip this part of the book. It is here for those who know very little about it so that they can get the ball rolling with their sales and reviews.

The first thing I do after I launch a new book is put it on 5 free days with KDP, and then I hammer promotion for a few days. (Actually, it's more like a few evenings while I'm bored!)

FACEBOOK PAGES/GROUPS

See the "reviews" section below for more in depth information. Below is a short list of generic book promo pages to join; titles are hyperlinked to the page. Be sure to follow the rules of each group if they have any! (Search Facebook to find groups, links included in Kindle version.)

CreateSpace & Kindle Self Publishing Matrix: – Started recently by yours truly! J

http://thinkclickrich.com/MatrixFB (Not open to all Facebook members!)

Become A Bestseller

Writers' Group

Awesome Free Kindle Books Here!

Writers Club

Free Advertising No Rules

Let's Review!

Free Kindle Books

Sell Online? Post it Here

Free Today on Amazon

Free Kindle Books

Be sure to investigate further to find pages that are dedicated to your niche. I suggest you do this sort of research when you have those moments of not wanting to write. You can get your Facebook fix and still be doing something productive with your time. The same goes for finding resources for the other types of promotion here, really!

GOOGLE+ COMMUNITIES

Again, a short generic list is below; see the "reviews" section for more info. Find groups in your own niche here: https://plus.google.com/communities. Once again, be sure to follow any guidelines before posting. (Search community names to find, links included in Kindle version.)

Writer's – Publisher's – Reader's MASTERMIND
Kindle Ebook Promoter
Kindle & eBook Writers And Reviewers
Self Publishing
Reading Deals for Fiction
Reading Deals for Non-Fiction
Reading Deals for Scholars
The Writers Community
eBook Publishing
Where Writers And Authors Meet
Writing

TWITTER

Have a Twitter account? Me too, and here's what I do…

I visit http://hashtagify.me/ and start getting creative. When I find something that is popular and related to my book's topic, I'll tweet about the book and work the hashtag(s) in somehow. No rocket surgery or brain science involved.

Also take note of what hashtags others in your niche are using and use hashtagify.com to see which ones are best. cycle through them and don't keep spamming the same messages constantly.

I also have a link to my author's page in my Twitter description. Go here to see it – https://twitter.com/ThinkClickRich.

REVIEWS

Yes, I know! Every single book out there on the subject of selling more Kindle books bangs on at you about how important this is and in my experience I can confirm they are right.

It is like pushing a boulder uphill trying to sell your book until you manage to get your first 4 to 6 reviews from what I have seen, so it does bear mentioning. No matter how well you have done your homework, you are going to have trouble selling if you don't have some good reviews in your corner.

Whatever your niche, there are likely to be groups or pages or whatever, that deal with it on Facebook, Google+, maybe tribes in Twitter or whatever they call 'em. Seek them out, make sure it is safe to post a link to your book and then do so as soon as you put it on a free promo.

When you post a link, introduce yourself and personalize your message to each particular page a little bit. Let the group know about your free days and ask for *honest* reviews. If you are scared to ask for reviews then there is probably more work needed on your book!

Do you have a family member who would be interested in the subject matter? Ask them if they will read the book and leave an *honest* review.

Got contacts or do you belong to a forum in the same industry or niche? Ask for an *honest* review.

NEVER ask people to give you a good review, only an *honest* review. With time, you will get the reviews you deserve anyway, so try to give good content. It will stand you in good stead for the reviews to come over the long haul.

Once you start getting positive responses from people, groups, and pages, make a spreadsheet listing them and their page URL.

Friend the people whom you start talking to and put them on your spreadsheet. Keep in contact if the conversation is interesting and allows for it.

One magic ingredient…

Ask them if there is anything you can do for them in return. They are taking valuable time out of their lives to read your book and then (hopefully) leave you a review. The more interaction you have and the better your relationship is, the easier it will be to get them to repeat this for you the next time you release a book. This is doubly true if they have called in a favor and you have helped them out somehow!

If reviews you have asked for are not forthcoming after a couple of weeks, give a polite reminder and then leave it at that. They may not agree with or even like your work so don't make them uncomfortable by forcing the matter. Push them and they may distance themselves from you or worst case, actually say they didn't like your book in their review.

This may all seem like a lot of work but trust me, that little spreadsheet will grow and it will help you get your first few reviews for future books more quickly, making it easier every time.

DEALING WITH BAD REVIEWS

While I don't have a lot of experience in this area (not too many bad reviews, thankfully!) I will give you a quick piece of advice from one of my experiences:

The first book I released was on long tail keyword research and how you could carry it out using free tools. When I published that book the tools listed were free and everything went pretty much hunky dory until one of the tools went to paid only.

So I get this review from a young lady who was furious about this, she gave me 1 star (rightly so!) and told the world how she had been duped. Anyway, I emailed the guy whose software it is and he told me it was going back to free. From there I clicked on the reviewer's link and lo and behold there were some contact details.

I emailed her explaining the situation and bought her a (cheap) eBook off her wish list by way of apology. Then I directed her to the once-again-free software. Now Vanessa, who is a trained English teacher and proofreader, has offered to proofread my books before they go live. What are the odds, eh?

I've also got one of the most shining reviews for that book from Vanessa and she sent me an email recently saying (in her own words):

"4-6 weeks after following your tips about 60% of my products are ranking in the top FOUR spots on Page ONE of Google!!! It's true! I nearly passed out when I saw it myself."

Not a bad result from contacting somebody who left a bad review?

Vanessa also gives me deep discounts on women's products such as handbags and jewelery when I need a gift for my wife. She doesn't know it yet, but she will once she reads this book.

Anyway, the moral is don't be afraid to reach out and set things straight if you have made legitimate mistakes in your books (or anywhere else). You never know, that person might even end up becoming a friend. (I'm almost crying here; I shouldn't write after a glass of wine.)

KEEP IT EVERGREEN AND FREE FROM OUTSIDE INFLUENCE

If I were to point out any regrets during my publishing journey so far, it would be the fact that I had written a book which revolved around some "thing" which was out of my control or would become obsolete further down the road.

If you write about software, how to use a particular piece of hardware, or anything that will (or might) lose popularity or change the way it operates, then expect to have to update regularly. (And during the period when (if?) you are updating it, expect bad reviews if you don't move quickly!)

I'm not saying there is no money in these markets, because there most certainly is, but it is more hands on than choosing evergreen niches.

Want an example?

"How to deal with difficult people." There will always be difficult people, right? If you need confirmation, just ask my wife.

The point is, you will never have to go back and change the teachings in your book, unless you find some new cutting-edge scientific approach. Even then you don't really *have* to update, because if what you are teaching works, it works! Nobody can change that and make your book redundant from the outside…short of eliminating all difficult people from the world, of course.

BONUS TIPS

OK, I suggest you run through the entire process of setting up your first Matrix before you use the first advanced tip. I could have included it earlier in the book but I think it is quite possible both of our heads would have blown up with the information overload.

ADVANCED ENEMY TRACKING WITH EMAIL UPDATES

You might remember, in the Matrix I gave you for this book I mentioned that Mr. Messick had increased his price. I knew exactly when he did this and could see what effect it has had on his sales ever since. If you too had this knowledge about your competitors, you could monitor their tactics and see what is working for them and then use that intelligence for your own ends.

You could avoid making errors that decrease your sales and revenue or you could copycat tactics that increase sales and revenue.

How about if you could get an email when their sales rank falls below a certain figure? You could immediately go and examine what they are doing to sell so heavily, using NovelRanks, Twitter and blog searches, right?

Here's how it's done:

Create an account for yourself at http://tracker.kindlenationdaily.com/

Once logged in you can create "groups" of books to track. One group I have, for example, is called "Kindle publishing" and includes all of the books I was analyzing in the Matrix for this book. Another is called "My books" where I keep tabs on my own books.

You can follow a similar setup for each Matrix you create. Put every book into it and then set up email alerts to come in when sales rank changes according to your specification.

Easy as pie!

GET KINDLE BOOKS FOR FREE (OR AT LEAST CHEAPER)

Another bonus of using this tracker is that when somebody drops the price of their book you can go get it cheap. Simply set up notification for low prices or freebies. I have a whole group dedicated to books I want to read set up this way… What a cheapskate, eh?

Even if you never use the Matrix, this book has probably just paid for itself with that piece of information.

My main reason for telling you about it here, of course, is for the purpose of tracking a book's performance when prices change. You can cross reference this information with NovelRank estimated sales if you are a real boffin, and look for signs that a price change has resulted in increased revenue or sales levels.

When you see the chart for a particular book at the Kindle Nation Daily tracker, scroll down to see records of all price changes.

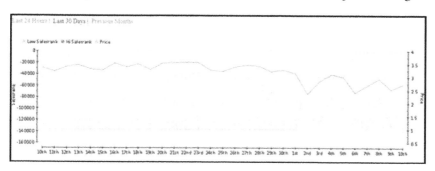

NOTE TO AUTHORS MENTIONED IN THIS BOOK

I would just like to say a quick thank you to all the authors I have mentioned in this book. Although you don't know it, a good few of you guys have helped me in my own journey as a self publisher and I appreciate that!

Those whom I have not read, I will. I know that all of us as teachers have our strengths and weaknesses when it comes to writing, research and of course promotion. I know I can learn something of value from each of you; I'm sure that anybody who has the know-how and bravery to put their name behind a book on such a challenging subject will almost always have good information which is of value to the self-publishing community.

You will all become part of my mastermind group in time so that I can improve my own work…Even if you are the enemy…

To you the reader, I suggest you also study the works of these authors. Keep learning and keep seeking out the answers to your questions!

I keep six honest serving-men
(They taught me all I knew);
Their names are What and Why and When
And How and Where and Who.

– Rudyard Kipling

CONCLUSION

The truth of the matter is that I am not sure if this book will outsell *all* of the other authors I have spoken about inside this book; some of them are fantastic at promoting outside of Amazon so nothing is set in stone with just this research.

What I do know is that this book *will* sell and give a lot of these authors a run for their money.

This is what I wanted to teach *you* to do all along. I hope I have been successful in your eyes and achieved this by bringing you unique information that is actionable without expensive software, by anyone, regardless of income.

How much of a beating I actually dish out to my "enemies" has yet to be seen... Exciting stuff, this self-publishing, eh? (Please let this book sell... Please let this book sell.)

*Cough... Moving on...

If you find yourself jumping around from one part of the system to another as you think of new things, don't worry! This isn't a strictly linear system, I often find myself doing just that myself.

I advise you to try to enjoy the process, allow yourself time to be inventive, especially on the title construction phase. Sleep on things if you (inevitably) start getting confused or tired. You might be amazed at what your subconscious offers up after a lot of concentration, followed by much deserved rest.

Never find yourself in the position of saying: "Oh… That will do!" Your book will be out there for years, one or two days extra spent working things out to the best of your ability may make a huge difference in the money your book makes, every single day of those years!

"The slow philosophy is not about doing everything in tortoise mode. It's less about the speed and more about investing the right amount of time and attention in the problem so you solve it."

– Carl Honore

Finally, for you to find out how I did with this book in comparison to the other authors, there is a blank column in the Matrix download with my name at the top. If you buy this book very early in its life, don't expect too much. It takes time for keyword phrase rankings to really kick in!

With a bit of time, and as a few reviews accumulate, (hint, hint: http://thinkclickrich.com/MatrixReview), go ahead, fill that column in for yourself and see how I did.

Thank you so much for taking this journey into the Matrix with me. Now, if you'll excuse me, I have to step outside with…

- A Ninja.
- Kindle publishing coaches.
- Book promotion experts.
- Programmers.
- The founder and CEO of the Strategic Positioning Press publishing house.

- SEOs.
- A Professor.
- An Amazon SEO specialist.
- A genius astronaut.
- 5 figure and 6 figure Kindle earners.
- A lecturer on nonfiction book publishing.
- An Amazon top 10 overall bestseller.
- A consultant who holds multiple degrees.
- 2 dark horses… I don't know who the hell they are!
- An editor in chief.
- The founder of SmashWords.
- That Steve guy whom I refuse to mention any more.
- An international bestselling author.
- That bloody Michael Alvear guy everyone keeps banging on about.
- AND agent Smith!

And you thought Neo had a hard time!

Once again, thank you for reading my book. Good luck in everything you do!

If I survive, maybe I'll see you in the Self Publishing Matrix Reloaded!

Chris Naish

CONNECT WITH ME

If you would like to connect with me on some of the social networks or other places, please hit the respective link below:

https://www.facebook.com/ThinkClickRich

https://twitter.com/ThinkClickRich

https://plus.google.com/+ChrisNaishThinkClickRich

http://www.pinterest.com/ThinkClickRich/

http://ThinkClickRich.com (my website)

Have problems or questions? If possible, ask in the Facebook group first so that others can benefit.

If it's of a more private nature, you can get me at my email address: Chris@ThinkClickRich.com

I look forward to hearing from and interacting with you!

EVER SEEN THIS IN A KINDLE EBOOK?

Finally, if you found this book helpful I would appreciate it very much if you would help me out by taking *a few seconds* to share the Amazon page with your friends by hitting a link below.

Note: *I'm beta testing this feature in this book so you are REALLY helping me by using this!*
How to do this for your books is shared in the private FB group!
This was originally trialled with share images in the Kindle version of this book and worked successfully. Here's your chance to help me test it in a real book!

Thank you!

Type a URL to Share

http://thinkclickrich.com/MatrixFBShares

http://thinkclickrich.com/MatrixTweets

http://thinkclickrich.com/MatrixPins

RESOURCES

http://thinkclickrich.com/MatrixReview – If you would very kindly like to leave a review?

C'mon! You know who I'm up against here! :-D

http://thinkclickrich.com/MatrixFB – Give & get help from your peers on Facebook.

http://thinkclickrich.com/Matrix-Download – Download the Matrix

http://thinkclickrich.com/Matrix-Categories – Ease choosing categories

http://thinkclickrich.com/Matrix-Books – Recommended reading

Lorecee's book proofreading/editing service – http://thinkclickrich.com/Proof-Edit

Lis's book formatting service: http://thinkclickrich.com/Book-Formatter

Amazon.com "Kindle eBooks" with book count for each category – http://www.amazon.com/b?node=154606011

Amazon.com "Books" with book count for each category – http://www.amazon.com/books-used-books-textbooks/b?node=283155

Amazon Bestsellers – http://www.amazon.com/
best-sellers-books-Amazon/zgbs/books

Amazon advanced search – http://www.amazon.com/
Advanced-Search-Books/b?node=241582011

Amazons metadata guidelines – https://kdp.amazon.com/
help?topicId=A294SHSUYLKTA6

FINAL CHECKLIST

I have been fortunate enough to have gained some insight from some helpful members at the Facebook group, into what slows people down when following the Matrix process while using this book. One of the members (thanks Rachel Bentley Ramey!) came up with the idea of putting a quick checklist here so that you, the reader will not have to go through this book multiple times when working through the system. (Why anyone wouldn't want to read this book several times is beyond me, but who am I to argue?)

1. Brainstorm single keywords.

2. Combine keywords into phrases while including variation and new ideas.

3. Type each phrase into Amazon (Kindle) noting new phrases while eliminating those that don't appear.

4. Find the books (closely!) related to your niche that rank for each keyword you list.

5. Skim competitor's titles for more keywords.

6. Repeat step 4 and 5 for any new books/keywords found.

7. Add all interesting competitors to NovelRank.

8. Look for top 100 ranking categories and decide on the best option. (Remember you can change later!)

9. Choose top competitors according to unit sales and income. (This will differ for different niches!)

10. Identify Red pills from keywords. (Little as possible typing needed for appearance in auto-complete.)

11. Identify long tails of red pills. (Hint: A,B,C etc before red pills sometimes helps!)

12. Hedge your bets: *Match red pills to best sellers, look for easy to rank red pills and include long tails where possible in final title construction.*

13. Remember that regular consistent sales, *may* point to a better keyword phrase than very high "out of the norm" sales. If the author is selling way above the niche norm check for external promotion, *before* relying on a keyword phrase.

14. Also add unique angle & pain points during final title construction.

15. Finally, decide on your 7 (5 for CreateSpace) fallen angels and keep them highly related. (Once again, they can be changed if ranking isn't good!)

MORE BOOKS BY CHRIS NAISH